The *Dance* between Joy and Pain

Dr Mansukh Patel & Rita Goswami RGN

First published in the United Kingdom in July 1995 by
LIFE Foundation Publications
Maristowe House
Dover Street
Bilston
West Midlands WV14 6AL
Reprinted in December 1995

ISBN   1-873606-07-9

Cover design and photography Regina Doerstel & Jeff Cushing
Illustrations by Lucy Claire Byatt

Printed by Offset Fifty Five, 30 James Road, Tyseley, Birmingham B11 2BA

Dedication

To all the members of the Life Foundation
for their immeasurable support
and to Mahatma Gandhi for his inspiration
and teachings.

Dear Reader

It is with great joy that we offer this book to you. Our hope is that it will become a guiding light in your life.

May we suggest that the first part of the book, **Understanding the Dance**, is read in 'short bursts'. Read a few pages and then close the book so that you can absorb what is written. Close your eyes, think about what you have read and let it settle in your mind for a day or so. Then come back to it and read some more.

All the techniques and exercises in this book are safe and effective. However, if you suffer from a physical condition which gives cause for concern, please consult your doctor before practising.

May this book be an inspiration, a guide and a friend to you always.

Contents

Foreword by Marcel Messing
Introduction

Foreword

As long as man is reaching other planets without changing his thinking and emotional behaviour, then he/she is not really a human being. When we can transform negative thinking and pessimism into positivity and optimism such as hatred into love, compassion and forgiveness; anger and jealousy into loving kindness etc., then we will be able to rise above the duality of life.

We can only do this through using the *power of the heart*. Learning to open up and cease to reject ourselves, so that we can begin to truly love the whole of life - for that is what we are. It begins with thinking and feeling with the heart. Christ said, **'Wherever is your heart, there is your treasure.'**

The essence of the ancient Scriptures is love and wisdom. Real love, known in every true religion, dissolves the feeling of 'me and you', between which hatred, compassion, anger and jealousy are born.

That is why Gandhi often spoke of the 'education of the heart'. An education in which you can really *feel* what love is, for spirituality begins when we start 'thinking' with the heart.

Dr Mansukh Patel and Rita Goswami are real heart teachers. When I first met them I was immediately struck by their compassion and loving kindness - qualities that make them stand out in the crowd. In this book they are telling us that no matter what pain is happening outside us, we have a great power **within us** - the power of the heart which we can use to transform negativity.

The Dance Between Joy and Pain is a friend. A precious guide for daily life. It is simple, humorous and direct. A heart power book that hopefully you will read with your heart.

Dr Marcel Messing
Teacher, Philospher and Author

How this book came about

A book that describes the dance between joy and pain can only be written from meeting the most intense experiences of life at first hand.

In the last few years we, together with our colleagues from the Life Foundation, embarked upon a series of extraordinary journeys involving 3,000 miles of long distance walking and 150,000 miles of air flights. We visited thirty-one countries and four continents - the most inspiring as well as the most disturbing places on earth. Our journeys have plumbed the depths of human experience from Jerusalem and Assisi, to Auschwitz and Dachau; from the slums of India to penthouse suites in New York.

This book has emerged out of the immense cry of the human heart. A cry for help, guidance and clarity about the nature of suffering and pain.

Introduction

Nobody goes through life without experiencing joy and pain and the misunderstanding of either can force us to **reject** one, or to **possess** the other. We have to master the dance that occurs between them, so that everything we do and every intention and ideal that we have is based upon how much we understand these two emotions.

Our research has shown that different parts of the world hold different parts of the jigsaw. Each part of that jigsaw gives insight into mastering the dance between pain and joy. The purpose of this book is to present people with a completed picture. One that offers real solutions to the 'problem' of pain.

The book is a distillation of techniques and wisdom that **really work** for people. Tried and tested, every story, statement and technique has already transformed the lives of thousands of people, and now **it has arrived at your door.** Enjoy the journey - and remember that we are with you all the way!

And nd could you keep your heart in wonder
at the daily miracles of your life,
your pain would not seem
less wondrous than your joy.

Kahlil Gibran

Contents

Understanding the Dance

The dance of life

There was an extraordinary story in the newspaper recently about a couple who were trying to get to a maternity hospital as the woman was in labour. As they sped through the country lanes the man's mind was full of panic and excitement and as he turned a bend, he just didn't see the black ice.....

The car swerved, narrowly missing a bus stop, crashed through a hedge and ploughed down a four foot embankment, eventually coming to a halt in a waterlogged field. Miraculously, although shocked and slightly stunned, they were both unhurt.

As the man fumbled for the carphone to ring for help he heard his wife's voice crying out, 'The baby's coming!'

Within five minutes the
ambulance arrived, just in time for the
paramedic to deliver their
beautiful little baby girl in
the front seat of the car.

As he held up the
tiny infant for the
parents to see -
amongst the
wreckage of their
car - they were
both crying with
joy!

The agony and the ecstasy.
The pain, the turmoil and the joy,
all co-existing side by side.

And this is the dance.

Pain and joy are married together
like man and wife.
Like day and night,
they are two parts of the whole,
each one inseparable from the other.

The yin and the yang
creating a perfect balance
and honouring of life.

Pain and Joy are similar, in that they both create an elevated sense of awareness which brings a profound clarity, so acute that we can only see what really matters in life.

All the unessentials drop
away like the skin
falling off
a snake.

If you have ever been in an accident, or in any situation where your life was threatened, you will understand this principle completely.

Suddenly, all the things we have been so concerned about dissolve into a pool of unimportance, leaving behind the only real essential which is **life itself.**

Joy brings us to respect life through a feeling
of gratitude for its nature.

> **Pain** also makes us honour life through
> the way it brings us to see **the uniqueness of life.**

> **We realise how much life means to us,**
> **and how much people mean to us.**

>> Again, the agony and the joy are there side by side,
>> always together like faithful friends.

Travelling through India, a bus load of American tourists came across a Harijan village. Harijans are outcasts, having 'no caste'. The great freedom fighter Mahatma Gandhi championed these underpriviledged people and re-named them 'Harijans', which means **'Children of God'.**

The Americans saw the little mud huts that they lived in, perched precariously amidst what appeared to be a rubbish tip. One man asked the driver to stop, and with tears in his eyes, he examined the faces of these forgotten people.

Then he realised that all of them - men, women and children alike - had brilliant shining eyes and a radiance of tranquillity.

6

He turned and looked at the stressed, anxious faces of his companions sitting in the coach. He could see that for all their wealth and comfort, they could not touch what the Harijans had.

Culturally we have been conditioned to focus more on the sorrow of pain rather than on the joy. **That is where the secret lies.**

How could the Harijans be so joyful, living in such impoverished conditions?

Their perception is different.

They have found the way to feel the joy within their situation, because they have not been conditioned to see their lives as unfortunate.

Just for a moment, imagine a man in a skyscraper flat in New York, his head in his hands. He has lost his job and his family and is afraid for the future.

He is experiencing pain

    and feels weakened and helpless.

Now imagine a Masai warrior, standing naked under a freezing waterfall at 4 a.m. It is part of his discipline of training to become a warrior.

He is experiencing pain,

    but he considers it to be
        a sign of his strength.

Pain can become a transforming experience

if we choose to let it.

We can retrain ourselves to see it with positivity
and optimism so that the joy that exists can become
apparent to us no matter what is happening.

Pain is not meant to be a **'pain-full'** but a **'growing-full'** experience. Something which leads us on in life and keeps us moving.

Marathon runners experience extreme pain at certain stages of their run, but they just keep on going, knowing they will break through the pain barrier into a heightened sense of awareness and strength.

10

They see the 'conditioned' pain as an indicator that they are about to make a breakthrough and with this attitude are able to surge forward and rise to new levels of energy.

**It takes courage and effort
and is a choice that we make**

Are the trees in the forest all straight and tall?
No! Each tree has its own pain - its own agony.
Each one twisted and gnarled in some way;
distorted by circumstances,
twisted, cut down, attacked by lightning,
its bark torn and stripped by animals.

A tree does not grow without pain and suffering,
but it grows to great majesty
because it has taken its pain and
allowed the whole process
to take place - without denying it.

Two men looking through prison bars,
one saw mud, the other saw stars.

You know, it's all about the way we choose to see things......

There was once a farmer who owned a very beautiful horse. One day, the horse decided to run away and his neighbour said to him, 'What a terrible thing to happen to you - such a great loss'. The farmer replied dryly, 'You never know, maybe good, maybe bad.'

The next day, the horse came back with another horse by his side and the farmer's neighbour said, 'What great good fortune, now you have two horses.' The farmer's reply was the same, 'You never know, maybe good, maybe bad'.

The next day the farmer's son fell off the new horse and broke his leg, to which the neighbour said, 'That's bad!' and of course the farmer gave his usual reply.

Soon after this, war broke out in the land and all the young men were conscripted into the army, except the farmer's son who couldn't go because of his leg. The neighbour said, 'What a great piece of luck,' and the farmer replied, 'You never know....'

There is so much truth in the statement, **'You never know.'** The reality for most of us is that we don't know where each event is leading.

14

Our predicament is such that life happens around us and events are not always in our control. We also know that the only thing we can control is ourselves and the way we perceive and receive life.

If we could see into the future we would probably view everything very differently.

*Every day we find ourselves facing a challenge -
of how we are actually going to live this day; and I believe
that our life doesn't have to be a life of struggle.*

*It can be one that rises like the phoenix from the ashes.
Arising with such great love and power, that all our fears,
all our anger, sadness and grief can be used as
energy transformed into love and compassion.*

We celebrate the birth of a child with great joy - but that birth does not come without extraordinary pain both to the mother and the child.

If there is fear and resistance, there will be contraction against the pain which can only serve to increase it, so much so that drugs become necessary to be able to cope with it.

If we can have the simple wisdom to relax and enter into the sensations we call pain, with awareness and an attitude of acceptance, something very beautiful can happen.

Then everything begins to look different.

We can create so much agony through our resistance to what is happening to us.

In childbirth, for instance, which is possibly one of the most painful experiences a woman can have, those who can relax into the contractions, flowing with and breathing through the pain, move with this most natural process and discover a richness within pain that can elevate them to a higher consciousness.

It is almost as though pain is a doorway through which we can enter to access a much greater potential - a deeper resonance within ourselves.

Pain is healing in process

When animals are in pain, they have an attitude of total acceptance and an instinct to do what is necessary to heal themselves.

They naturally stop eating and withdraw to a quiet place so that nature can take its course. In other words, they do not resist the process that pain instigates.

This is wisdom!

It's such an important thing to recognise that pain and joy are

    side
        by
            side

like the inbreath and the outbreath,
    so that we can integrate them into our
        experience of life.

There is documented evidence regarding many people who were imprisoned in concentration camps during the war, which indicates that the majority of survivors were those who were best able to totally embrace their suffering.

Accepting what they could not change, they focussed instead upon finding meaning for themselves and others around them.

20 Those who could not accept their situation and what they had lost in terms of property, position and power, were simply unable to rise above their suffering, as if they had already died within themselves, even before entering the gates of the camp.

*S*uffering is not a punishment,
it is a gift,
but like all gifts,
it depends upon how we receive it....

Suffering can turn

'I was walking along the sands of life, feeling miserable and full of pain, hard done by, neglected and without a friend.

My battered shoes were torn and full of holes, cuts and blisters stung my feet. The burning sun beat down upon my face as the sweat poured down my skin. I felt my suffering was extreme.

Then I came across a man sitting on the ground - with no legs. Only rags covered his scorched skin and his eyes spoke of a depth of suffering I could not even imagine.

Suddenly, I was filled with compassion for this man, and in that moment my own pain seemed to totally vanish and turn into deep appreciation for what I actually had. Never mind a dirty pair of battered shoes - I had legs and feet to put them on.'

**Pain and suffering can turn in an instant
with a simple change of perspective.**

Finding the way to turn it is one of the greatest discoveries of life, because our suffering is the great frontier presented to teach us what we have to learn in life.

Contents

Mastering the Dance Part I

Contents

Body/Heart/Mind Technology

Why Body/Heart/Mind Technology?
Gentle Movement
Hand gestures
Visualisation
Affirmations and Sound
Walking with Awareness
Breathing Consciously
Body/Emotion Relationship

Body/Heart/Mind Technology methods look at a human being from the physical, emotional, intellectual and intuitive levels.

Physically, our health and emotional balance, dynamism and energy, are intimately related to the balance of hormones within the endocrine system. An imbalance in this system, or in any of the seven physiological systems of the body, will create not only a physical effect but also an emotional one.

27

It is important to realise that the mind has the strength and power to control the body. The physical and mental perspectives are well known to us. However, there is a third aspect which is unknown to most people and that is **the perspective of the heart**. The heart is so powerful that it can completely rebalance the physical, emotional and mental aspects of a human being. This we can call the **heart master.**

Instead of fighting with uncontrollable and unmanageable emotions and mental states, we can put our energy into **understanding the workings of the heart master,** and discovering how to fully apply its power in every situation.

It is a hidden power, however, and we need to be able to activate it in order to access the energy that can transform negativity within us into an experience that actually empowers our life.

From a physiological point of view, heart power is found within the powerful field of energy that surrounds and drives our heart. It is the same power that keeps it beating more than a million times in one lifespan. It is the central driving force of the human body.

On the mental and emotional level, heart power is the gateway to intuition which is the faculty that allows us to flow without resistance to life.

When our intuition flows well, we experience no problems in anything we do, and things naturally work out for us. The aim therefore of all **Body/Heart/Mind Technology** methods is to access this heart power and make it a central strength in our lives.

The most amazing thing about heart power is that it is so easy to access, requiring only our focus and attention to activate it. If everyone could realise this, then healing the world would be a cinch! The first obstacle to overcome is **disbelief.**

29

Believe that it exists, then move towards using it.

Body/Heart/Mind Technology shows you how.

Body/Heart/Mind techniques put you in touch with how to use your whole self and your surroundings as a complete breathing, walking, healing package.

Practically BHM Technology methods will ask you to:

1. Gently move the body
2. Use hand gestures
3. Develop creative visualisation
4. Use sounds and affirmation
5. Breathe consciously
6. Walk with awareness

Why?

Gentle movement stretches and detoxifies stressed muscles and organs; re-aligns the skeletal system; relaxes the nervous system; boosts the immune system; replenishes vitality; assists efficient energy management.

Hand gestures act on the body's subtle energy systems to recreate a balance of energies, hormones and nerve impulses. Hand holds have been used in the Indian sub-continent for centuries to transform the hormonal changes that produce emotions.

We all make hand gestures every day to express our feelings, but how many of us know that when we make a gesture, we are empowering the thought behind it? For example, Churchill used the 'V' for victory to emphasise his determination to win the war. The national lottery symbol also empowers the will to win and the famous 'thumbs' up sign adds strength to a conviction that something is 'great'.

31

Visualisation develops mind strength, using the power of the mind to direct energy towards healing, regenerating and replacing old, unwanted thought patterns. Management and sales teams utilise this technique to achieve commercial success.

Affirmations and sound are keys to transforming the way we feel, by altering the way we think. The sounds we make and the words we speak, powerfully affect the way we feel on every level, and the way our relationships develop. For thousands of years, sound has been used to create particular body/mind/emotional environments. For example, we have all experienced how a favourite piece of music can change the way we feel.

Breathing consciously calms the emotions and energises the mind. It activates the parasympathetic nervous system which in turn reduces stress and anxiety and creates a sense of calmness and control.

Walking with awareness not only provides exercise, but also enables us to get in touch with ourselves and can set free potential energy that builds mental and physical stamina and endurance. Walking in nature provides a sense of freedom and space and it often allows creative thoughts to arise and take root. Walking also transforms energy from one form to another (such as anger to kindness) and allows us to relax and let go of stress. Seen in this way walking becomes a therapy in its own right.

Body/Heart/Mind Technology methods recognise and work with the intimate relationship that exists between the emotions and the body's organs. This interplay is a well known science in Eastern and indigenous peoples' medicine. Emotions are a form of energy, which, if they cannot find an outlet or a way to transform themselves, can become trapped in a particular part of the body .

33

The emotions affect the body just as a breakdown in our physical well being affects our thoughts and attitudes. For example, when we are feeling ill and our body is low in vitality, we will often begin to have negative thoughts. Similarly, if we think negative thoughts, sooner or later this will become reflected in the body. *(See page 252)*

As heat conserved is
transmuted into energy, even
so our anger controlled can be
transmuted into a power which
can move the world.

M K Gandhi

from anger
to creativity
and dynamism

It was the night of Channukkah, bitterly cold and dark as the 200 members of the peace convocation gathered around the gates of the Auschwitz camp. Most of the people there were Jewish and had direct connections to the place and the events of the past.

They had been chanting Jewish songs, and there was a strong feeling of bonding in the group as they each lit the nine Manorah candles they were holding.

36

I looked around me and marvelled at the faces of these people who had travelled such long distances and with such expectations of the event. I could see their tears reflected in the candle light, at the same time remembering and imagining the people who had passed through those gates.

That such a thing had ever taken place......

How often Channukkah would have been spent there - uncelebrated. The flames danced in our eyes and the sound of Yiddish songs rang in our ears. Each one of us wished that for every flame lit, at least one soul could be set free.

For myself, a non-Jew, I could feel deeply the significance of this gathering of prayers. As the last strains of a song faded softly, a young woman next to me suddenly cried out, 'How could they do this to my mother and father?' She was a child of Auschwitz survivors and the pain of it blazed in her eyes. I turned to put my arm around her and say, 'It's alright', but she would not be consoled.

'Why shouldn't I be angry?' she said indignantly.' Don't try to take that away from me, because my anger is the strength and power that I have to make sure that Auschwitz never happens again.'

The steel in her words spoke of the mighty, transforming energy of anger that fires us into action when it is directed. Without direction however, its expression can be destructive because anger is not harmonising. As all life is based on harmony, whenever harmony is betrayed, we will have to pay the consequence of that.

Mansukh

38

When we can use anger to teach ourselves about a disharmony within us, it becomes a positive experience.

Anger is my shield when I feel threatened by life and by people.
It is my armour against a hostile world. It hides my hurt and pain
that I choose not to feel.

**In reality it offers no protection at all, as it
actually opens the door to what we fear.**

Anger is the strength I believe I have,
the fiery weapon that I use to gain control
of things and to get my own way.

**If we can let go of using anger to manipulate
events, we can access our true power.**

I feel angry when my expectations are not met.
Are my expectations realistic or reasonable?

Sometimes we react with anger when we feel threatened. When we are not safe with our hurt and fear, we will retaliate. If we can share our hurt with sincerity, we will find the anger dissolves.

People mirror what is going on inside us.

As anger is generated in the same place as creativity, it may be time to acknowledge that energy and to open to a higher level of self-expression within ourselves.

40

It does not matter at all what the **cause** of our anger is, but what we choose to do with it **really matters**. Anger needs to be understood and harnessed if it is to be transformed into **creativity** and **dynamism**.

Refuse the gift

The Buddha once visited a village in India, where people flocked to listen to him. One young man became so spell-bound that he lost all sense of time, forgetting his duties on his father's farm. The father sent his other son to find him, but he also became captivated by the Buddha's words. Soon another son was sent and the same thing happened.

41

The father furiously made his way through the village to find them himself. Pushing his way through the crowd, he confronted Buddha with an angry tirade of abuse, accusing him of enticing young people away from their responsibilities instead of teaching them the value of hard work and loyalty to their parents.

The Buddha smiled and said, 'My friend, if I come to visit your house bearing a gift and you accept it, whose is it?'

'Mine, of course,' the father replied, a bit taken aback.

42   'And if you were to refuse the gift, who would it belong to then?' The man was very irritated by this point but replied, 'Yours, but what has this to do with anything?'

Buddha then said, 'Your gift to me right now is anger, and I refuse to accept it. So it remains with you.'

If people are getting angry around you, take the example of the Buddha and **decide not to take it on.** If you confront anger with more anger, you will never find a solution to the challenge. You are only trying to suppress the anger that is in front of you. 'If you can shout, I can shout better!' It takes you nowhere.

If you really want to learn from life, ask yourself sincerely,

43

' Why is this anger being sent to me?'

The universe is always guiding us to recognise what we need to see about ourselves. If it is happening a lot, it may be useful to examine which part of you is attracting it. Did your parents get angry with you as a child so that you are used to that high energy feeling around you? Perhaps you are holding anger inside you that needs a creative expression?

Frustration, irritation and impatience are the first rumblings of the storm of anger. We may feel that all our efforts are being blocked and we're just not getting anywhere. Frustration is a good sign that there is a lot of energy available which simply needs a new avenue of expression. Redirect your energy.

Attitude
44
1. Be very positive about feeling frustrated!
2. See it as a positive motivator to becoming more effective.

Action
3. Think of new and different ways you could achieve your aim.
4. Look to someone who has achieved what you aspire to and ask their advice.

Ten Step Plan For Dealing With Anger

1. Respond skilfully: Act instead of reacting.

2. Resist: That powerful impulse to express the anger.

3. Take Responsibility: My anger is my own creation, no one
else's. Remember that nobody can make you angry and you are
never justified in blaming anyone else for it, **no matter what they
have done**. Others only act as a catalyst.

45

4. Throw out Righteousness: But I am right! You may well be, but
sometimes it is just too painful to be right. Communicate with
others in the way you would like to be spoken to. How would you
like to be treated?

5. Question yourself: Do I really want to feel angry? Will it change anything? Is it worth giving up my peace of mind for?

6. Redirect it through: Running, tennis, squash, cycling, swimming etc. Anger enables us to run faster and further! Use your anger to improve your health!

7. Creativity: Painting, singing, dancing, pottery, Tai Chi - any form of self expression. Why not dig a pond!

46

8. Use your Breath: Watch the breath coming in and out. Bring in peace on the inhalation and allow it to spread throughout your body on the exhalation.

or

9. Breathe in: Hold the breath and count to ten. Breathe out slowly and gently, letting go of your frustration.

47

10. If you are in a situation that is making you angry: Get up and go outside. Walk around the block affirming in your mind, 'I will walk until this anger goes away.' You'll be surprised how quickly you will be able to let go of it! (Especially if it's raining!)

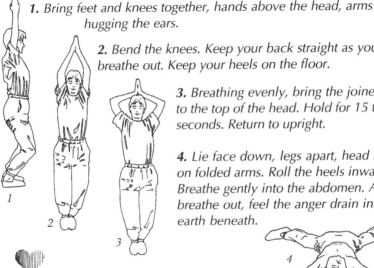

1. Bring feet and knees together, hands above the head, arms hugging the ears.

2. Bend the knees. Keep your back straight as you breathe out. Keep your heels on the floor.

3. Breathing evenly, bring the joined hands to the top of the head. Hold for 15 to 30 seconds. Return to upright.

4. Lie face down, legs apart, head resting on folded arms. Roll the heels inwards. Breathe gently into the abdomen. As you breathe out, feel the anger drain into the earth beneath.

4 8

The Lion Heart

Alternate Nostril Breath

Place the right thumb gently on the right nostril, the index and middle fingers between the eyebrows and the little finger gently against the left nostril. Close the left nostril with little finger. Breathe in through the right nostril. Replace the thumb. on the right nostril, release the left and breathe out.

49

Breathe in through the left nostril, then close the left side, release the right nostril and breathe out. This is one round. Repeat up to five times.

This gesture balances the right and left hemispheres of the brain, calming the angry storms of the mind.

The Gesture of Tolerance

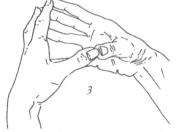

Join these three fingers

50

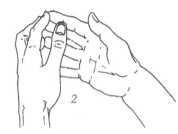

Join middle and index fingers

Hold each gesture for one minute in sequence to diffuse anger, frustration and impatience. Focus on the colour pink.

This gesture dissolves anger.

Join all the fingertips together

Love really makes a difference

A very creative teacher in America one day gave each of the children in her class three pinned ribbons upon which she had written, 'Who I am really does make a difference.'

She asked them to wear one and give the other two away to someone that they admired and to ask them to pass the other ribbon on in the same way. One boy gave his to a man who had been helping him with his project. He was a very high powered businessman - someone who rarely had time to stop and think about such statements. But for some reason, the gesture touched him very deeply.

As he drove home that night he was thinking about who he could give the other ribbon to and as he walked into his house, he saw his son sitting on the sofa. Without thinking, he went up to him

and said, 'Son, I know that I hardly
ever see you, and I never tell you
how much you mean to me, but I
want to give you this ribbon so that
you know that who you are really
makes a big difference to my life.'

To his amazement, the boy started to
sob uncontrollably. His father put his
arms around him and held him until
he could speak. Finally his son
explained, 'Dad, I was planning to
kill myself tomorrow, because I was
sure nobody cared about me.'

Don't hesitate to tell someone you love them today.

Come to the edge he said.
No, we are afraid.
Come to the edge he said.
They came, he pushed them....and they flew.

Guillaume Appollinaire

from fear
to courage
and strength

After attending a Peace Conference in Jerusalem, we crossed over the border from west to east to visit a French peace worker who had been living in the region for some fifteen years.

Her house, which she calls 'The Ark', is in a notorious part of the West Bank which, unbeknown to us, had been the target of a dawn raid by Israeli security forces.

56

Arriving at the outskirts of Abadiz, we were met by an atmosphere of fear and tension and the young soldiers manning the road block looked very anxious and tense.

We chatted to them in an attempt to break the tension, and it soon became clear that they were very reluctant to police what to them is a terrorist area. They questioned why we wanted to enter such a zone, and when we replied that we had a friend there, they said, 'Nobody has friends there'.

Fear for their lives had made them completely unable to see the Palestinians as people with human rights, hopes and aspirations, just like theirs. In this sense fear is very isolating and alienating and can stop us from relating to people at a human level.

Rita

57

Fear is an imagination - not a reality.

Fear can be a paralysing phenomenon. It's directly proportional to your own imagination, so that if you think it's big - it is. If you think it's nothing - it is.

Fear holds us back and prevents us from acting appropriately in life. When we can actually **confront our fears,** we see that they have no reality - no basis in fact.

58   It's only the thought of what **might happen** that creates the fear.

The only thing that can take fear away is to **meet life face to face** without any assumptions.

Remember that your deepest fears guard your greatest strengths.

Sasamori is a Buddhist monk who has led several peace walks into war zones. When he meets a potentially fearful situation, he has always found that his experience has been the exact reverse of what he had anticipated. From this he realised that he should **never make an assumption about anything.**

His teacher sent him to do a peace walk in Nicaragua where there had been civil war for some time. He linked up with a Christian peace group and hundreds of villagers who also wanted to walk with him.

Two days before the walk began, they received a warning from the Contra soldiers that if they stepped on to their territory they would be killed.

Sasamori decided to definitely continue with his plan to walk through the war zone, but he didn't want to take anyone else with him.

However, they all expressed the same sentiment. 'Our people have died for war, we might as well die for peace'. They walked into the conflict zone fearlessly and miraculously not a single shot was fired at them.

He realised the power of offering the very highest to God - his own life. By putting your life on the line for peace - before your fear of death - you are protected, because there is a greater power at work.

60

We asked him if he ever felt afraid and he replied, 'Yes, I am always afraid and have to pray very hard when going on walks. Something always protects me. Facing death, the rug is taken out from underneath you. You take your own personal support away and allow God to support you.'

Fear of death is the root cause of all fear.

There is a universal law that states that 'what is natural to us is naturally acceptable'

We seek happiness because it is our real nature. Likewise, we long to be eternal because it is natural to us and we fear death because we think it is the end. When we can realise and believe in our eternal nature and learn to trust in the perfect harmony of the way the universe works, we realise that there is nothing to fear

61

If you can get over the fear of death, you won't fear anything.

Believe in the power of life!

Fear is a very powerful energy which can cause us to run at incredible speed when under threat and to do things that previously seemed impossible.

It is not an enemy as such, for without it we would not know when to avoid danger. It teaches us not to roller-skate on cliff edges or dive into shark infested waters.

62

So it is not something that needs to be destroyed. We simply need to understand its nature and what its message is to us. If we make it an enemy, it will enbed itself more deeply in us.

> **Never take no for an answer.**
> **You can do anything if you're willing to ask**
> **and remember - it takes ordinary people**
> **to do extraordinary things.**

Understanding transforms fear. Look into the cause of your fear. Where's it coming from?

Trust dissolves fear. Trusting that we will not be destroyed - no matter what happens. Trusting that life is always supporting us in whatever we do.

If you have to stand up in front of 60,000 people to give a speech, the universe will give you the power and strength to do it. If you **trust** this - then you will deliver your speech. If you **do not trust** - then fear becomes your master and you will be a trembling jellymass! So **trust life** and go for it!

63

Acknowledge you are always safe and fear will go away

If we avoid situations that make us feel uncomfortable, we are encouraging fear to dominate our lives.

Fear, anxiety and worry are indicators to us to be prepared to deal with what is about to happen.

1. Imagine a fearful situation. What do you need to do to prepare to meet it?

64

2. Visualise yourself going through the situation totally successfully - without fear and full of confidence and courage.

1. Locate your fear

There is a part of your mind that is fearful and a part that isn't.

Take the part that is fearful.

Breathe in and be aware of it.

Breathe out and surround it with
the part that is not fearful.

65

Ask yourself: What's the worst thing that could happen?'

Imagine it in detail. In your mind, take it all the way through to its conclusion. Is it really as bad as you thought? Facing the fear, head on, means it can no longer have power over you.

2. Cultivate your inner strength. Know you are a powerful being by creating a purpose that overrides your fear. Resolve to make life as you would like it to be. For example 'I am going to make two thousand people happy/smile over the next five years, and then work out how you're going to do it.

3. Honour and nurture yourself in the best way possible to short circuit all the things that feed fear into you, like the media.

66

4. Live in the moment - forget the past and the future.

5. Breathe in a sense of peace and then breathe out fear.

The Gesture of Openness

2. *Raise your right hand in front of your face and spread the fingers wide. Slightly move the hand like a leaf swaying in the wind. Perform for at least 30 to 60 seconds.*

67

1. *Rest your left hand, palm upwards on your left knee.*

This gesture eradicates fear and allows openness to establish itself.

The Gesture of Courage

Raise your open hands shoulder height, palms facing forward. Draw your hands back towards your chest and feel the shoulderblades squeezed together. Hold for at least 90 seconds.

68

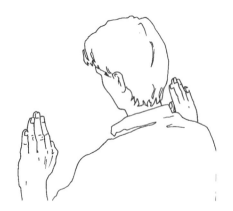

This gesture draws out the courageous lion within.

1. Interlock the hands behind your back.

2. Breathe in and pull the arms up behind you. As you breathe out start to bend forward from the hips, keeping the arms straight above. Breathe naturally for 30 to 60 seconds.

3. Soften the knees, slowly breathe in, uncurling from the base of the spine. Release the hands.

6 9

1

2

3

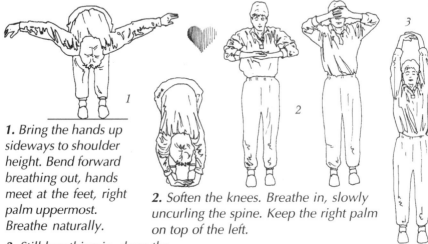

70

1. Bring the hands up sideways to shoulder height. Bend forward breathing out, hands meet at the feet, right palm uppermost. Breathe naturally.

2. Soften the knees. Breathe in, slowly uncurling the spine. Keep the right palm on top of the left.

3. Still breathing in, draw the hands slowly up the front of the body. Raise them up above the head. Hold. Look up slightly.

4. Breathing out, bring the arms down to shoulder height and continue the sequence. Repeat for three minutes.

*S*ilence is the richness of the soul.
Loneliness is its poverty.

May Sarton

from loneliness
to oneness

*L*oneliness does not feel natural,
and does not resonate within us;
but we have to realise that friendship is not passive;
it requires our active participation to make it flourish.

The Peace Formula

Have you ever been alone? Truly alone?

Walking into the highlands of Snowdonia, we touched upon it.
Alone in a bleak landscape, with no trace of trees, buildings or
features of any kind to separate us from the horizon.

Initially, it is a relief, especially after the hustle and bustle of the
Midlands. Aloneness can be a place where we gather strength and
clarity to give meaning to our relationships and our lives.

75

Taken too far, 'aloneness' turns into 'loneliness' and instead of
gaining strength and energy, we find ourselves losing energy,
vitality and enthusiasm for life.

How is it that with so many people living on this planet, one of the greatest diseases that besets our humanity at this time is that of loneliness?

It is not natural for human beings to be alone and separated from each other in the way that we find ourselves to be in our modern day society. It seems as though loneliness has been imposed upon us by our environment, but we all need to recognise that we have created it in ourselves through:

Fear and mistrust of each other.
Selfishness in not wanting to share with others.

These two things have created a contraction within us which means that we are no longer expanding out into life, but instead, withdrawing into our little 'safe' spaces.

We each create a space around us that we feel protects us from the things that we fear.

If we really want to resolve loneliness, we will have to confront our fears:

Of opening up to others.
Of sharing ourselves - our thoughts, feelings, time and energy.

The law of attraction states that we will draw to us circumstances according to our most predominant thoughts. So what are we thinking?

See The Peace Formula - Oneness

Ask yourself:

How do I feel about opening up to other people?

Do I make time for people to share my time and energy with?

Do I close myself off from others to feel safe?

78 Is there a protective barrier around me that I have created to keep
people out of my space?

Am I willing to let it down and to let people in?

Affirm: **It's safe to open up to other people**

Generosity is the key:

1. Every day, write a few lines on a postcard and send it at the end of the week to someone who you know would really appreciate it.

2. Give someone an unexpected gift - for no reason at all!

79

3. Try to get out and make a connection with people.

See The Peace Formula - The Power of Generosity

Heart Expansion Breath

80

1. Stand with feet apart, knees soft. Cross the arms with palms facing outwards.

2. Breathe in and draw the arms up in front of the body and above the head.

3. Hold for a few seconds. Breathe out, bring your arms back down ready to repeat the movement.

4. Perform at least three times.

*F*ullness, warmth, expansion. I touch
the unlimited nature of myself and feel safe inside.
A part of everything and everyone.
Separation dissolves into the mists of illusion
from whence it came.

and then there is .....

solitude

solitude

Henry David Thoreau lived for two years in a small cabin by the side of Walden Pond in complete solitude.

He was cured of loneliness through his recognition of his intimate relationship with everything in nature, from the animals and birds to the plants and flowers, and to the pond itself. As he began to understand the nature of solitude, he realised that people feel lonely through a misunderstanding of what loneliness and separation actually are.

Loneliness does not arise because we are not near people, but from a feeling of separation from the self.

In his book 'Walden' which he wrote during that time he said, 'I can stand as remote from myself as from another'.

If we believe that we are all alone in a hostile world, we will always feel lonely. 'Alone' is a word people use to describe a state of being solitary, but broken down it actually says **'All - One'** - the truth of life.

For we are connected together by the force of life that runs through every living thing. Like beads on a necklace, of every shape and type, but all connected nonetheless.

85

When we can allow ourselves to become aware of this thread of life it is simply impossible to feel lonely.

In the fullness of silence we touch the union we all long and search for in each other. Make time to be still enough to feel this union.

See The Peace Formula - Unity

'The simple difference between loneliness and solitude is whether or not you are in the present moment......'

How to be in the present: Do not try to plan for the future or think about the past. Just be here, now, in the present.

86

Hold your hand in front of you, index finger pointing up. Put all your attention on to the fingernail.

Just look at it - and look at it - and look at it.

Believe it or not, you have just spent a few moments in the present!

The Feather Breath

Breathe in stillness and in this way you will discover solitude within yourself. Be aware of your breath coming in and out.

8 7

If you can imagine a soft white feather in front of your nose, breathe so softly that the feather is not knocked away.

Affirm: I accept everything that I am

Gesture of Solitude

1. Sit comfortably on the floor or on a firm chair.

2. Interlock your fingers as shown so that the thumbs just touch firmly.

3. Keep your eyes half closed, focussing downward slightly. Breathe naturally and peacefully making the exhalation at least twice as long as the inhalation.

4. Focus the mind into the natural stillness that arises at the end of the breath.

Rising above it all

Whilst we were walking through the French Pyrenees, a huge bird suddenly flew up from the ground beside us followed by two black crows. What was clearly a young eagle flapped clumsily along the ground, while the crows were frantically chasing it.

90 We watched as the great bird rose up and slowly began to climb, quite obviously not used to it. The crows followed in hot pursuit, continually diving at it and pushing and pecking at its body.

Then the crows darted out of sight leaving the eagle circling clumsily, rising slowly into the sky. Suddenly, they came back like two black arrows and divebombed the eagle, who dropped fifteen to twenty feet. The attack was fierce and relentless as the crows kept repeating their divebombing tactics. Then quite unexpectedly, some strength seemed to come into the eagle and it began to climb higher into the sky. The motions of its wings became powerful as it rose, steady but sure. Very soon the crows could no longer keep up, and were forced to leave. The eagle now took on a new look. We stood mesmerised as the great bird circled our heads for several minutes - now very high up in the sky, before soaring at great speed across the valley, soon to be lost out of sight in the mountains.

It was quite a spectacle to witness, and one which clearly demonstrated what it is we have to do in order to overcome the doubts and fears, anger and despair, that are constantly nag, nag, nagging us all the time.

At any moment, our true strength and greatness can rise up inside us. It can take us so high that nothing and no-one can ever touch us. **This is our potential** and like the eagle, we may have to take many knocks before that majesty will emerge and take over. **One certainty is that it will, if we believe in it and do not allow the knocks to bring us down.**

You need to give yourself permission
to be what you want to be.
There is no greater danger for a
human being than self condemnation,
because it takes away the very essence of power
that can make everything happen for you.
It takes away inspiration and all possibility of ever succeeding.

The Peace Formula

from inadequacy
to self worth

James gazed out of the window at the great oak tree that stood watching over the valley beyond. He loved that tree because it emanated strength and continuity in a world full of changes and uncertainty. It stood like a rock, reassuring and comforting.

He thought about his life and how so many circumstances had occurred to bring him to this point now. His job had been a good one and although very stressful it had made him feel important and 'somebody'.

He had always wanted to be somebody, but now he just felt useless. Losing his job was bad enough, but he never thought Jill would leave when the going got tough. 'I worked so hard to feel good enough as a human being,' he thought, 'but now I can see it was all just a cover up for what I really feel deep inside me.'

He wondered if the Oak ever felt inadequate. 'No, it is content being a tree, never striving to prove itself to anyone,' he thought. And what a great strength it had in just being itself. He got up and walked out across the valley, sitting himself down under the tree.
Looking up into the branches, he could feel how small he was in comparison and as the pain burned through his body he sighed.

It felt so good to stop running from that feeling. Nothing to prove any more and no-one to impress. 'Perhaps now I can find my own greatness.'

I'm more than adequate just being me.

95

The whole of society is motivated from the point of view of the power game.

'I am better than you,' or, **'You are better than me'.**

We are each one of us full of power and no-one is more powerful than another. However, some people have accessed their inner power and believe in it, while others believe that they are weak and power-**less.**

> **If we accept that people have power over us,**
> **it drains our strength away.**

In the Native American tradition it is believed that a person is empowered when they are **on the right path** - following their true purpose in life.

To have power, we need a vision that is **greater than us** and which embraces the whole - not just ourselves.

   The higher our vision, the more empowered we will become.

Inadequacy is not believing we have the ability to accomplish what is in front of us.

9 7

Ask yourself:
1. Is it possible I really do have the ability and that my perception of myself is inaccurate?

2. What would I really like to do in my life, short term or long term? Set an agenda and draw up a plan.

Action:
1. Every day, spend 5 minutes visualising yourself achieving your aim. This process is particularly effective if done **last thing at night** before falling asleep.

9 8 **2.** Find someone who is accomplished in the area you aspire to and find a way to learn from them.

> **Affirm:** I am a total success
> I am a strong, confident and successful person
> My potential is unlimited

See The Peace Formula - My Relationship with Myself

Build a strong self-image: Successful thoughts create a successful life.

Spend: Time every day building up an image of yourself as you would like to be. See yourself achieving what you want to achieve.

Search: For things to acknowledge about yourself. Make a list of things you are good at.

99

Focus: On what you have achieved in your life, not what you have not achieved. Acknowledge yourself for past achievements, however small.

Remember: As you think, so it shall be.

Heart Hug

100

1. Imagine you are holding a tree, your arms hugging the tree at shoulder height.

2. Visualise the strength and power of the tree flowing into you with each in breath and filling your whole body on the out breath.

3. Become a tree, strong and powerful.

Affirm: **I am strong and powerful**

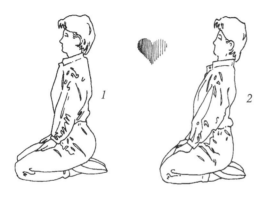

The Sun Breath

1. Sit in on your heels. Use a cushion or sitting stool if necessary.

2. As you breathe in allow yourself to lean back about 5 degrees drawing your awareness to the abdomen as you do so.

3. Breathe out as you slowly lean forward about 5 degrees, making the sub-vocal sound 'whoo'. Draw your awareness to the heart. Perform five times.

Transforming tragedy

In 1992, we visited Prague during a marathon lecture tour spanning thirty three countries and eighteen months. It was there that we learned about the life and work of Marie Uchytilova.

In 1945 when the world was celebrating the new peace, Marie was twenty one. One of Czechoslovakia's most promising young sculptors, the war had made a deep and lasting impression on her. In particular, she was appalled by the fate of the thirteen million children who had perished during six years of war.

Marie was determined that a tragedy of such vast proportions should not be forgotten, but that it should be used to awaken the love that all nations and peoples share for children.

Marie believed that this wealth of deep human feeling could be channelled to deter future wars, and to inspire nations to find peaceful ways to resolve conflicts.

It wasn't until 1969 that Marie found a concept to accomplish her vision. It was based on the events of 1942 in the small village of Lidice in Czechoslovakia. In June of that year eighty-two children of Lidice were taken from their parents and the village razed to the ground in a reprisal for the killing of a senior SS Officer. The children, varying in age from 1 - 16, were taken to a concentration camp and gassed.

Marie decided that she would sculpt each of the eighty-two children, creating a group composition of slightly larger than life figures. So powerful was Marie's conviction that for twenty years, without a day's rest, she poured her love into her 'little ones'.

Marie finished her life's work just before her death in 1989 and it has been acclaimed as a masterpiece. Marie, with the eloquence of a master, has laid bare the terrible vulnerability of childhood. In their innocence, each of the figures calls out to us for protection and love. No-one can remain unmoved in their presence.

The more we understand the oneness of life, the more we must accept responsibility for events like those of Lidice. This responsibility leads us to a sense of urgency - an urgency to heal, to make peace, to build with the fabric of our lives a world which cares too much to allow such tragedies to happen again.

Marie felt that urgency and acted on it in the only way she knew how - by creating a work of art of such sensitivity and beauty that it can heal hearts and minds and transform tragedy into triumph.

Rita

*A*nd you would accept the seasons of your heart,
even as you have always accepted
the seasons
that pass over your fields.

Kahlil Gibran

from crisis
to transformation

Life is always working to evoke transformation within every aspect óf creation.

It is not enough for an acorn to stay a seed - as beautiful as it is, because its potential is to become a great oak tree that will sustain and uphold human life forms on this planet. The crown of creation - human beings, cannot escape this wonderful process; but we can resist it!

108

The natural world surrenders, accepts and yields to the forces of nature; but for some reason we fight, object, rationalise and complain. If an acorn were to resist the process of change it would never become a mighty tree.

Can we not surrender and yield with the same dignity that the acorn has? Can we not move with the powers that be, instead of against them?

One of our dearest friends is a lady who had been married for almost 30 years. Angela was very beautiful and David clever and successful. She was only seventeen when they met and had never had any other relationship, and he was a young medical student of 23. Theirs was a loving and quite special partnerhip and they knew it. They had two wonderful children who were now following brilliant careers of their own, a home she had lovingly moulded into a palace, financial security and social prestige. They had it made.

But this perfect life was suddenly to become shattered for them both when David became involved with a much younger, dynamic woman who was to become the catalyst for the greatest crisis of both their lives. Angela was devastated when she found out because David constituted her whole life, and she knew nothing else except living for him, caring for him, devotion to him.

Perhaps it had all been too perfect and too comfortable. The pain she felt was almost unbearable and many times she felt she would not get through it. She just wasn't used to things going wrong and was ill-equipped to deal with the agony she felt inside.

Betrayed, angry, humiliated and bereft, she didn't know where to turn.

Today ....only a year later, Angela is a completely different woman. She is living alone, very happily, surrounded by loving friends with a diary full of appointments. No longer does she sit and wait for the man in her life to come home to light up her day.

No longer is she **living for just one person.** She is travelling around the world, meeting new people and feeling powerful in her own right, not an appendage to someone else's success.

111

In short, she feels free for the first time in her life and she is discovering herself - it's a revelation to her! She now feels that what happened was 'right' and 'meant to be' and even a 'blessing', because she would never have had the courage to leave the comfort of a life that was actually stifling her......

How did she do it? Read on.......

Angela needed to:

1. Accept what had happened to her. This is the first and biggest step, because acceptance plays the most important part in transforming crisis. It means we are not fighting what is happening and like the acorn, can yield and embrace the situation and all the feelings that accompany it.

112 **2. Let go** of her husband. It gradually dawned on her just how much her attitude of clinging to her husband had created the situation. She realised how important it is to let things go, to let people go and to trust that if something or someone we cherish is removed from our life then something better will come.

3. Keep her heart open to love and therefore to the pain she felt, in order to use it to her advantage. Once we can accept what is happening, we also need to be able to accept the sensations of pain that accompany it, allowing the feelings to simply come and go like the waves of the ocean. The pain will pass, just as a wave does.

4. Trust that what was happening to her was in accordance with **a greater plan for her life.**

5. Be grateful for the opportunity to experience life more deeply. Gratitude allows us to eradicate the biggest bugbear of all time - the 'poor-me' syndrome because self pity creates so much unnecessary suffering.

6. Forgive the people concerned.

Initially she did not feel accepting, trusting, open hearted, grateful or able to let go, let alone forgive!

We suggested two powerful methods to help her:

1. The Salutation to the Four Directions
The Ancients used this salutation to align themselves with creation. Whenever they needed strength or power to achieve a particular purpose, they would call upon the forces of nature from the four corners of the earth. In performing the salutation, we are acknowledging that we are not alone in life but interconnected, and we are allowing help to come to us.

This sequence is the panacea for everything! Whatever you are feeling, the salutation will turn it to your advantage.

2. Silent sitting

When we make time to sit with ourselves, we begin to become aware of the tremendous power we have inside of us. In silence, the strong feelings that crises evoke can act as a doorway to the deepest part of ourselves. The part that is all wise and all knowing, completely unaffected by anything that happens to us.

Angela's success in turning her crisis into a personal triumph **lay in her willingness to take on both practices** of silent sitting and saluting the four directions.

115

Every morning, she sat with a candle and focussed her mind on simply breathing in and breathing out, or using a guided meditation tape. Whenever she felt overwhelmed by pain, grief, anger or fear, she practised the salutation - using the energy to propel herself forward into a greater sense of strength and self empowerment.

Why you should perform The Salutation to the Four Directions if you really want to change your life.

The secret to success lies in our ability to allow movement, breath and affirmation to work in harmony with each other. **Movement** awakens the primordial resonance within us because we were born to move. **Breathing** is the bridge between the mind and the body and its essence is the secret of life. **Affirmations** feed not just the mind but also the body. What you think today is creating your tomorrow.

116

On the mental and emotional level, the salutation brings us back in touch with ourselves, allowing us to act as our intuitive self. We are able to see situations and people from a clearer perspective - from four directions. We call upon the positive qualities that enhance our interactions with life to help us to create new patterns of behaviour in order to let go of the past and to move *forward.*

On the physical level, this salutation removes energy blocks within the whole body which creates a healthy free-flow that replenishes and revitalises the body's energy system. It enhances the natural grace and flow of the body, stimulates the innate healing mechanism within us and tones and strengthens leg muscles, releasing tightness in the hip girdle.

117

On the spiritual level, it awakens us to the phenomenal potential we possess as human beings and teaches us how to assess it effectively.

It helps us to recognise our true nature and to establish our inter-connectedness with the whole of life. Last but not least, it will create a feeling of total peace and tranquillity amidst the storm of life.

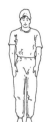

Stage One: *Facing North, begin by stepping out to the right and placing the right foot, heel first, onto the floor. Bending at the knees, gently lower into a squatting position.*

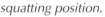

118

Gathering energy from the earth with both hands, raise up by straightening the legs and draw the energy up. Turn the hands at the heart and take them above the head.

Open the arms in a wide rainbow gesture and then draw them back and down to heart level. Repeat on the other side, stepping out with the left foot.

Stage Two: *Reach the arms out to the right hand side, to draw in the quality of* **Acceptance.** *The arms travel up and over the head and circle down and back once again to the outstretched position.*

119

Imagine: The colour blue.

Affirm: I accept all that life offers me.

The Salutation to the Four Directions

*Draw the hands back to the heart and hold for a moment, thinking about the quality of **Acceptance**. Repeat on the left side.*

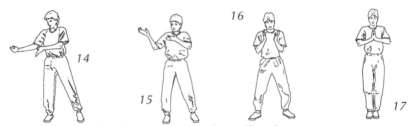

You have now saluted one direction.

*Now pivoting on the ball of your right foot, turn to the right, facing **East**. Repeat the sequence, drawing in the quality of **Gratitude**.*

> **Imagine:** The colour **Red.**
> **Affiirm:** I am grateful for everything.

Pivot once again to the right, now facing **South** *and draw in the quality of* **Letting go.**

> **Imagine:** The colour **White.**
> **Affirm:** I let go and flow with my life.

Once more turn to the right. This time you will be facing **West,** *and draw in the quality of* **Trust.**

> **Imagine:** The colour **Green.**
> **Affirm:** I trust that everything is for my ultimate good.

A tape is available should you like to have further guidance for this sequence. Simply fill in the card insert and send it to the address shown.

Loving touch

In India many years ago a young woman lived with her husband and mother-in-law. The old woman was constantly complaining and bickering about everything and anything.

After a few years, the daughter reached a point where she felt she simply could not take any more and that she was losing her mind. She knew she couldn't say anything to her husband and in desperation devised her own plan to get rid of her. She went secretly to a medicine man to ask for a potion that would slowly kill her mother-in-law.

The wise man gave her some herbs to massage into her mother-in-law's feet every night, and assured her that after a couple of months she would mysteriously pass away without pain. The young woman went away filled with joy at the prospect of ridding herself of the bane of her life and dutifully applied the lotion to the old lady's feet telling her it would help her to sleep.

Over the weeks the old lady began to complain less and less, and even to smile from time to time! The daughter thought it must be the effect of the poison, and happily continued applying it. However, after two months the old lady seemed to have undergone a personality change. She was so happy and pleasant to be with. The young girl even found that she had begun to warm towards her, so much so that she began to regret what she was doing.

She woke up one morning filled with remorse and rushed to the medicine man to beg him for a potion to reverse the effect of the poison. He smiled knowingly and then told her the herbs she had been applying were just aromatic - nothing more and that the dramatic change had come about simply as a result of her taking time to touch and care for the old lady.

*I*nside hate is love.
Inside love is hate.
Inside this hate is an even deeper love.

Mansukh

from hatred
to love

We joined the world peace walk from Auschwitz to Hiroshima during the walk's Middle Eastern leg through Israel. We met a young Palestinian called Johar who told us that he had been incarcerated in a sweltering desert detention camp for almost three years. One day, an Israeli soldier spat in his face and all he wanted to do was to vent his hatred on his tormentor, even if it cost him his life.

126

Suddenly, through his blinding rage, Johar heard the words of his friend Yvette who had said to him, 'If you want to win against hatred you have to be big enough **to give of yourself** when faced by it. Mentally offer your enemy a rose'.

With this memory came a surge of strength flowing into his mind and body. Not a strength to strike out with, but **a strength to love** in the face of hatred. Across the chasm of antagonism which separated them as human beings, Johar looked at his tormentor and in his heart, offered him a rose of peace and friendship.

To his amazement, tears of sadness and remorse welled in the young soldier's eyes. He looked down in shame and then slowly turned and walked away.

For Johar it was a triumph! Caught in a situation which debased captor and captive, the human heart had proved itself mightier than aggression and prejudice.

127

Rita

If we hate someone because they have done a terrible wrong, we actually empower their ability to do wrong. We can choose to forgive and to love them and this actually has the power to change them.

Hatred is the end point of a very long process. It is an action that is disguising the fact that there is a very deep hurt, and **the way out is to act in a very positive way.**

To be able to retrain your mind away from hatred, you need to feel fulfilled by something. Selflessness, which is **action that is done with no selfish motivation** - is fulfilling by its very nature.

As Saint Francis said, **'It is in giving that we receive'** - and he knew what he was talking about!

Hatred begins by disliking something or someone. It is the very opposite of love, where we hurt so deeply that we cannot face ourselves and so make a choice to act destructively towards the source of our hatred instead. When we hate however, **it actually hurts us** more than the other person, and often they are completely oblivious to how we feel! The whole experience goes on inside **us** - and is **our own creation.**

129

Hatred is very destructive to us, never mind anyone else! When it becomes severe, it's important to do something about it. When we choose to take even one step back towards love, all the forces of the universe converge to help us, simply because loving is our purpose in life.

If you are feeling hatred, you'll have to decide whether to stay in this self destructive cycle, or to move out of it.

The Gesture of Compassion

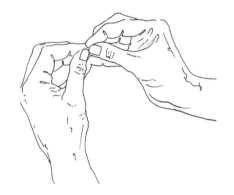

130

Hold the hands close to the heart with all the fingertips joined together. The thumbs face inwards towards the body.

Hold for a minimum of one and a half minutes focussing the awareness on the heart.

**This gesture empowers compassion.
Practise daily when sitting.**

The Swinging Pendulum

1. Stand with feet apart, hands on hips.
Knees soft.

2. Breathing out,
bend forward from the hips and relax
arms towards the floor..

3. Breathing in, feel the expansion
of the spine. Relax the buttocks.

4. Relax the spine with every outbreath.

5. Gently swing from side to side
on each outbreath, and swing towards
the middle on each inbreath.

Releases negative energy from the base of the spine.

131

This exercise is performed imagining the person you are in conflict with sitting opposite you. Your partner mirrors your movements.

1. *Sit comfortably. Raise your hands to shoulder height, palms facing outwards touch. Imagine a flower in between the partners's eyebrows. Breathe in and as you breathe out, see the flower opening. Breathe in and see the petals close. Three times.* **Affirm:** *I am peace.*

132

2. *Now allow both your hands to lower to heart level. See the flower in the centre of their heart. Breathe in and as you breathe out the petals open. Three times.* **Affirm:** *I am love.*

The Mirror Image

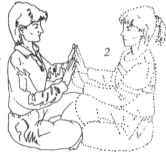

3. Now lower your hands to your knees. Right hand faces down on top of your parter's upturned palm. Left palm faces up with your partner's hand on top, palm down. Imagine a flower in the area of their navel. Repeat the same process breathing in and out three times.
Affirm: I am truth.

133

4. Raise your hands to heart level once again and imagine a ray of pink light passing from your heart to theirs.
Affirm: We are one. I choose love.

Warning: This exercise will turn hatred into love!

If you ever feel sad,
agitated
or in despair,

light a candle.

It will remind you of the
wisdom of your highest self
and the power of your own spirit

and brings a sense of peace and calm.

The lamplighters

Whilst we were in Canada, the last stop in our world pilgrimage, we met a remarkable old man who turned out to be the ex-chauffeur to Air Vice Marshall Dowding, during the second World War. He told us a fascinating story about the power of light.

During the darkest time of the war, when the Allies were retreating and things were looking bleak for Britain, Air Vice Marshall Dowding appealed to the British people. He asked everyone to light a candle or lamp every night at the same time. They were asked to focus all their love and prayers onto that candle and to visualise their loved ones in active service being surrounded by that same light and protected by its strength.

Very soon after this practice was put into operation, Hitler moved his forces East towards Russia - and the rest is history. The tide of the war turned dramatically in our favour.

When the Allies took over SS headquarters in Berlin, they found a series of papers documenting the events of the war. It became apparent that during one particular week that year, the specialists in defence firmly believed that the British had a secret weapon that they were directing towards Germany. The reason they thought this was because from that specific date, all the German decisions and activities seemed to fail.

That date coincided exactly with the week that everyone in Britain began the lamplighting movement.

Rita

*A*ccepting others as they are
brings a wonderful freedom to
your own mind.

The Peace Formula

from judgement
to *compassion*

Righteousness, which is at the root of all judging and critical traits, is a major source of suffering in life. It really comes from a sense of inadequacy and fear, and therefore a need to feel 'better than' other people.

Prejudice is a big problem for people. We simply do not realise how much we **hurt ourselves** by having attitudes of prejudice

140   about cultures, languages and beliefs.

When we are secure with who we are,
and certain of our own direction,
there's no longer any need to judge others,
or put people down in our own minds.

If I point a finger at you - there are three fingers pointing at me.

It is so easy to judge other people for the way they are or the way they behave. We always assume that our way is the best and only way, don't we? We are often too quick to condemn others for being other than we think they should be.

What we do not realise of course, is that **judgement, criticism, condemnation** and **prejudice** in any form actually opens the door to sadness, pain and grief in our lives.

141

The old American Indian adage, not to judge a man until you have walked a mile in his moccasins, is based in deep wisdom. If we really knew how other people operated, where they are coming from and all the influences they have been exposed to, we might have more **understanding** and **compassion** for them instead of judgement.

If we can always operate from the heart, we are less likely to make judgements.

What does that mean?

142

It means living from a point of compassion, care andunderstanding, open and receptive to new perspectives. The closest we usually get to it is in those fun moments in life when we let go of the burdens and problems and our true nature pops out. Playing with the kids, diving into a swimming pool, sliding down the helter skelter or whatever.

We **can also use movement** effectively to focus our energy into activating our heart centre in order to bring these noble qualities out of their cupboard.

See exercises with the heart power symbol for surefire methods!

Judgements often come from old pain and resentments we hold on to and a need to feel 'better than' others in order to feel good about ourselves. Judgement and all its counterparts are a cage that we put ourselves into - and freedom from judgement is real freedom.

Getting ourselves out of this cage is one of the most powerful ways to bring about a sense of stability and self empowerment in our lives. Instead of leaking out energy through judging, criticising and condemning, we will find we are building inner strength and stability through acceptance, tolerance, compassion and love for people.

143

However! We are so programmed to judge others that it takes a lot of conscious effort on our part to be able to climb out of our cage.

Self judgement

When we judge ourselves it drains our energy and power away. It can lead to a serious condition known as **self hatred**, which is very destructive and leads nowhere.

Appreciate yourself unconditionally

144

1. Build your self worth on a basis of all the small successes you have ever achieved in your life. Success is a constant practice so **never think about any failures** - just let them go.

2. Forgive yourself for not being perfect.

3. Think of ways to improve yourself, but concentrate 90% on the solution and only 10% on the problem.

4. Most importantly - Forgive yourself for making judgements!

Choose to love and choose to love again.

Climbing out of the cage!

Realise this:
1. Everyone is unique and different.
2. Everyone has a right to be the way they are.
3. Judgements isolate us from others and also from ourselves.

Practise this:

1. When you feel a judgement about someone coming on - stop! Try to imagine what it would be like to be that person.
2. Ask yourself: Do I want to feel separate from others and therefore from myself?
3. Go into your heart and say, 'I choose to love this person instead of judging them'.
4. Forgive people for not being as you would like them to be. They are only human!

The Gesture of Compassion

Hold the hands close to the heart with all the fingertips joined together, thumbnails
146 *facing inwards towards the body. Hold for at least 90 seconds focussing the awareness on the heart.*

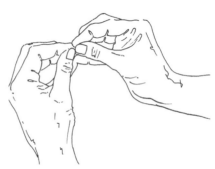

**This gesture empowers compassion and non-judgement.
Practise every day in your silent sitting.**

The Gesture of Friendship

With hands in front of the heart, hold them so that backs of fingers touch, pointing down. Thumbs touch pointing towards the heart. Hold for at least 90 seconds.

147

This gesture dissolves the energy of conflict.

Maximilian Kolbe

During the spring a large number of our team assembled in Auschwitz for a peace vigil of prayer and fasting. There we met Mr Yukiewiewicz, a survivor who had witnessed quite a spectacle during his time in the camp. This is his story....

If anyone ever escaped from one of the camps, the SS would automatically sentence ten innocent prisoners to die. On one such occasion, a young man in his thirties was selected and he broke down in tears, begging for his life saying, 'I have a wife and children - what will become of them?'

Normally, if anyone dared to speak up or step out of the crowd, they would be instantly shot. Consequently, when an older man came forward and addressed the SS Fuhrer, everyone froze. Terror hung in the air as they each awaited the inevitable.

Such was the impact of this man's fearlessness that the Fuhrer was compelled to listen as he offered his own life in exchange for that of the younger man. To everyone's amazement, the SS Commandant agreed.

His name was Maximilian Kolbe, a Franciscan priest and he was led to the hunger cells with the other nine victims to stand without food, water or sleep until death. Up until the moment he died, he kept singing hymns, leading prayers and caring for everyone around him. After two weeks, the SS injected him with poison and his life was ended.

Mr. Yukiewiewicz described the effect that this immense sacrifice had upon the people in the camp. 'At that time we were all completely numb to any feelings.

We dared not feel emotion because it was too dangerous. We all believed that we had become bereft of human feeling. When Maximilian offered his life in that great act of courage, a surge of deep and heart felt feeling went through us all. It gave us hope, courage and great great strength. It illuminated our lives in an indescribable way. It still continues to touch people even today just to hear the story.

150

That moment when I witnessed his immense sacrifice, has become the most important moment of my life'.

**The answer to pain
lies within the pain itself.**

Mansukh

*L*ove does not fail you when you are rejected,
betrayed, or apparently not loved.
Love fails you when you reject, betray and do not love.

Therefore do not stand off from relationships.
Be vulnerable, be wounded when necessary
and endure that wound or hurt.
Do not punish the other in love.
Communicate - do not dissociate from one another
or fail to grant each other the knowledge of love.

Mansukh

from rejection
to self love

Navsari train station in India, is an experience never to be forgotten. Teaming with life, a jam packed mass of colours and smells, full of all kinds of different people from street sellers and businessmen, to mothers with screaming children. The whole of humanity seems to be represented in that one place.

154

We watched the tactics of the young children who constantly ran up to people with outstretched hands and huge imploring eyes, begging for money. More often than not they were rejected, and sometimes quite aggresively so. These beautiful children would just smile and try again - completely undaunted by the negative response. It's almost as though it is a part of the job to be rejected!

Watching this scene alerted me to the fact that the human spirit has a great capacity to overcome rejection. You couldn't help but admire their indestructability and high self esteem - the keys to overcoming rejection.

Rita

When we give our heart and love to someone and they appear to reject us, it can be devastating, because it can feel as though the very quality of who we are is threatened; leaving us with nothing and nowhere to turn.

What is seldom understood is that no-one can reject us unless we have first rejected ourselves. Likewise, if we have come to love and accept who we are, people's behaviour towards us cannot destroy us. So the real issue is **self esteem** and when we can work with that, we will be able to see situations **as they really are.**

155

We need to give ourselves the love and recognition we feel we need from others and not to allow life's circumstances to destroy us. With wisdom we can use them to bring out the very highest within us.

Self love is the master key to all emotional pain. But how? The truth is that if we do not love ourselves, then it is without a doubt the real problem in our life from which **all other problems spring.**

When we can change our attitude towards **ourselves**, everything else will change as well, for our life is a reflection of the way we feel about ourselves.

156 ## Heart power technique:

1. The next time you feel rejected by someone or something that has happened to you, find a quiet place to sit, close your eyes and focus your mind on the area of your heart.

2. Experience the pain you feel there.

3. Imagine a great power-house of love inside your heart and consciously activate your heartpower.

4. Allow the love to envelop and soften around the pain. You could imagine a coloursuch as pink around it.

5. Say, 'I love and accept you - right now - as you are,' to yourself, over and over again with the same feeling you would towards someone you love very dearly.

6. Allow the power in your own heart to melt the pain away.   157
Focus on the love - not the pain.

Spoil yourself: Go out and buy yourself some nice clothes! You need to feel good about who you are.

The solution to pain lies within the pain. If we can have the courage to sit with it and feel it, we have an opportunity to heal the **root** of the problem so that we do not have to continually create rejection.

So often our aversion to pain means that we don't give ourselves the chance to touch the joy and freedom it contains.

158   **By accepting it,**

        going inside it,

                embracing it,

                        pain naturally changes its form.

See The Peace Formula - Living Beyond Conflict

The Gesture of Innocence

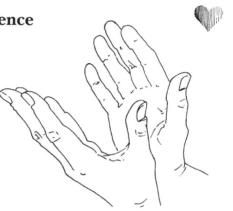

Press the heels of the hands together in front of the heart. Fingers are spread apart and shaped like a lotus flower. With eyes closed, focus on the colour green in the heart. Hold for at least a minute.

159

This gesture opens the heart and soothes the pain of rejection.

160

1. Rub your hands strongly together until warm.

2. Now separate the hands a little and simply draw the hands together and apart in a wave like motion.

3. Slowly allow the wave like movement to become wider until you no longer feel the energy between them.

4. Hold this position for a moment, and then bring the right palm on to the heart and the left palm on to the right hand. Close your eyes and feel the peace.

This movement transforms rejection into an attitude of 'respect'.

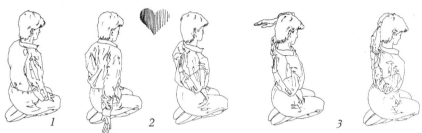

1. Sit in the kneeling position.

2. Bend your right arm behind your back, bending at the elbow.

3. Now bring your left arm up and over your shoulder to meet the right hand (or near!) Keep the head facing forward.

4. Hold for 15 - 30 seconds breathing naturally.

5. Repeat on the other side.

N.B. If your hands do not meet, you can use a sock or piece of cloth to bridge the gap.

In the same way that rain water does not stain the lotus leaf, this hand hold will strengthen and protect your heart centre so that rejection cannot hurt you.

161

A spirit of hope

We were led into the gas chamber as part of an organised tour and the first thing that struck us was the emptiness. Hollow, stark and cold. it was hard to imagine how people had felt as they were led into that place 50 years ago - to die.

The physical darkness reflected the feeling of those times - the heaviness and oppression. When everyone had left we stayed behind, standing in the darkness with only the shaft of light from the door to illuminate us. We knew we couldn't leave it as we had found it.

I struck a match and lit the candle I had in my hand, gently placing it on the crude little altar in the middle of the floor. Something inside me sighed.

The flame did not fill the room with light, but it felt as though it had welcomed something in. A spirit of hope and optimism - a silent presence that gave us a feeling of thanks for life - and a deep moment of connection for those who had passed through there.

No longer a feeling of sadness or despair, but rather one of the bizarre contrast between knowing what had gone on in the past, the darkness and the very powerful effect of simply lighting a candle.

A reminder of the powerful light of the human spirit that shines on in the darkness, and cannot be destroyed by anything or anyone **- no matter what they do**.

> **It is better to light a candle**
> **than to curse the darkness.**
>
> *Chinese proverb*

Heavy inside, with no energy or enthusiasm,
life weighs down upon me.
I am crushed and feel unable to rise up above it all.
Sinking, falling, nowhere to turn.
No-one can help me.
I feel so alone...

*from depression
to self empowerment*

Two hundred kilometres between North Wales and the
Midlands, in the middle of winter - on foot. The young men
carried tents and sleeping gear on their backs all the way. An
exploration of persistence!

As we watched our hardy winter LifeWalk team return, the
brightness in their eyes spoke of the barriers they must have gone
beyond.

166

This is the perseverance we need for overcoming depression.

In one of our seminars we came across a very special lady called
Betty who has been blind nearly all her life. She is one of those
people who is so full of joy and laughter that you just love to be
near her. During the seminar however, she suddenly burst into
tears while I was describing a movement sequence. 'I can't see

what you're doing', she cried. 'I can't see you'. It was quite heartbreaking to hear her expressing her pain at being blind.

She later explained to me that she had been fighting depression all her life and had always managed to stay bright and positive but every now and again she got caught out. **'I always have to make the decision to get out of it, and each time it is my direct choosing'.**

Betty has good reason to be depressed because her situation will never change. The Life walkers are young and strong, easily able to overcome barriers, but Betty is an older woman, blind and frail.

167

The strength she has is her constant perseverance in overcoming the depression that has always threatened to spoil her happiness.

Rita

Life can become overwhelming at times. Circumstances can occur that lead us to feel we have no control over our lives. When we feel resigned to being powerless and therefore helpless to change things, it can create a shut down within us that we call depression. It is as though the very vitality and exuberance of our spirit have been locked away.

168 When this happens we are actually living from the lowest level of our being. It is a very lonely place to be and also, surprisingly, very sweet. There is something about depression that we enjoy and feel reluctant to let go of.

We hold on, almost as though it's a raft in a treacherous sea. Why? Because **it offers a refuge** from having to take responsibility for things - **a bolt hole to hide in.**

Once we can realise that we have created it as an escape from overwhelming obstacles, we then have two choices:

1. To stay depressed and enjoy it.
2. To examine a new way to look at things and consider that there may be different and more positive ways of dealing with the obstacles in our life.

Ask yourself

169

a) Am I eating foods that may be affecting the way I feel?

b) What is my attitude to life? Am I willing to see things differently?

c) What am I feeling that I am unwilling to express? Am I angry about something? Can I find a way to express what I feel?

d) Build up a profile of strength and only empower that, not your weaknesses.

Gratitude is the best attitude!

Openly expressing gratitude for what we have in our life, both good and bad, has the instantaneous effect of changing the way we feel.

1. Every morning before your start the day, think of three things you are grateful for in your life.

170

2. Openly express gratitude for the challenges in your life.

Affirm: **I am grateful for everything in my life**
            I am grateful for the way I feel
            I am grateful for every challenge that comes my way

See The Peace Formula - The Power of Gratitude

The Su Breath

171

1. Sit in the thunderbolt with the palms joined together.

2. Breathe in, raise your hands up to your mouth.

3. Breathe out, extending the arms forward, turning the palms outward and keeping the index finger and thumb in contact. Breathe in.

4. On the next out-breath, make the sub vocal sound 'Su', bringing the arms around sideways and down to the sides. Feel the expansion in the heart space.

The Gesture of Acceptance

With right index finger touching left thumb, take hold of middle, ring and little fingers of the right hand with the four remaining fingers of the left hand.

172

The right thumb sits like a child between its parents. Hold the hands with fingers pointing upwards. Hold for at least sixty to ninety seconds. Focus on the affirmation:

I am willing to let go and be happy.

From the front

Joy is a natural expression
of the laughing human heart.

Dance to freedom

Just as the wash-down was completed they heard the unexpected sound of the siren announcing roll call. They had no opportunity to even dry themselves before being marched out into the freezing night to fall in line for their numbers to be counted.

174

As the commandant began to slowly count the men, Moshe became aware that his feet were becoming slowly welded to the snow beneath. He could see the water on his body beginning to turn to ice and a deep chill began to penetrate his body. The roll call seemed never ending and then they heard the voice of the commandant announcing a discrepancy of one which meant they would have to do it again. Fear gripped his heart as he saw several of his friends falling to the ground.

As he felt himself wanting to give in and escape into oblivion he suddenly heard the voice of his Rabbi coming from inside him. 'Moshe! Do not yield! You must not give in! You must stand up!' The voice gave him energy, but he soon began to doubt his ability to endure and the voice came again, 'Moshe! You must sing and you must dance! This is the only way to survive.'

As he vaguely perceived men collapsing all around him he then became aware of a great surge of heat and energy within him and a strength rising up as he determined to fight. By sheer force of will he prised open his lips and invoked a sound from deep inside him. At first it was barely audible, but then as it broke free from his lips he could hear a song of freedom emerging loud and clear. It was the song his Rabbi had taught him as a little boy. A song of survival, faith and empowerment.

He knew he must dance, but his feet were stuck to the ground. He focussed all his will and strength to the soles of his feet, concentrating on the right foot first. He could feel his heel slowly lifting, and bit by bit he prised it from the ground, leaving the skin behind. Singing loudly he once again willed his left foot to move as, oblivious to the pain, he began to propel his body forward to dance. At that moment, he heard the commandant announcing the end of the roll-call. Moshe danced back to the barracks, singing his song of freedom at the top of his voice. All he left behind him were his red footprints in the snow....

Moshe is still alive today. He lives in America with his family. Every Sabbath he gathers them around him to celebrate the freedom he experienced on that freezing night in the concentration camp. They sing and dance to that same song of freedom that helped him to realise he was invincible and untouchable and to this day he is still teaching the importance of singing and dancing as a way to find freedom from suffering.

*Y*our pain is the breaking of the shell
that encloses your understanding.
Even as the stone of the fruit must break,
that its heart may stand in the sun,
so must you know pain.

Kahlil Gibran

from grief
to renewal

Our travels into Uganda, where a large percentage of the population are HIV positive, showed us grief in its rawest form. We went to work with Aids helpers in the Malaga Clinic where the tragic victims of Aids were all around us. Numbed into silence by their inevitable fate and the loss of many of their relatives, most of them were just one in a long line of family members who were waiting to die.

180

We were amazed that the helpers were so cheerful and able to give hope and encouragement to these people, surrounded as they were by tragedy. We could see they had realised that where there is love, faith and hope, fear leaves and what seemed impossible becomes possible.

Rita

Grief comes like a shadow across our lives, in the wake of the loss of loved ones or dramatic change in our circumstances.

Initially it's like being in a dream where everything seems unreal and hard to relate to. This is because shock and grief actually dissolve the boundaries of who we think we are, leaving us feeling disorientated and confused.

181

Something that was very much a part of the foundation of our life has been removed and we can feel quite lost - unable to find a point of reference.

We may find it difficult to be a mother, father, friend or bread winner. At this time life is difficult to face and feelings of loneliness, anger, resentment and bitterness will swamp our already tired emotional system.

Grief is a process of **disintegration** of everything we recognise to be ourselves and a gradual **re-integration** that will *always* lead to a very positive change within us. How can we assist the re-integration process?

1. Affirm all the good and positive aspects of your life, like your children, family and friends. Just because one thing has gone in your life, it doesn't mean it **has all gone.**

2. Try to focus your mind on **what you do have** instead of what you have lost.

3. Deliberately think about the best things. Affirm: 'I have a wonderful family and good friends'.

4. Do not cut yourself off from people, because you really need them right now. Be with people as much as you can and try to keep the conversation very positive.

5. Above all, **leave nothing undone** between yourself and the person or situation that you are grieving for. Talk it through in your heart and affirm all the good things about that person or situation.

One woman was so angry because her son had been run over by someone who had gone through a red light. Her anger seemed to her the only defence against the terrible pain she felt. Within a couple of years she had contracted cancer and she knew it was because of the rage that she refused to let go of.

A friend advised her to talk about her son and the things she loved the most about him. As she did so, her anger dissolved as all the love she had for her son came to the surface. The anger and the love could not co-exist.

What we have to do is to re-establish our boundaries. How?

Firstly by re-defining **where we are right now,** and **what we are doing.**

For instance, saying to yourself, '**I am in the bathroom and I am washing my face!**' (Make sure you are!)

184

'**I am in the kitchen and I am making a cup of tea.**'
This will help to bring about a sense of security within you.

It is also very important to **give yourself something very positive to do.** Don't sit around thinking about what has happened too much, because it can become a problem for you.

Decide to **work with** the plethora of emotions and not to get stuck in them.

Grief is nature's way of healing the pain of loss. Initially the numbness of shock is nature's anaesthetic from the full impact of the loss. Then the rush of emotions may begin to come through.

Feelings of anger towards other people involved in the event, or for being left all alone.

Fear and guilt that you didn't do enough or weren't there at the important moment. This may be tinged with remorse and regret for things said or unsaid.

Sadness often comes in waves until we can fully accept what has happened.

Give yourself permission to feel all these things, letting them wash over you. Accept them without resistance, so that they can just pass through on their way out.

Don't hang on to them and then it will be a healthy process without which there may be problems in later years in the form of illness or depression.

186

Welcome and trust the process, which leads finally to the peace of acceptance and letting go.

Why do we cling to grief?
Sometimes we can hold on to grief for many years and there comes a time when we have to let go. It can become a habit because the pain is so familiar and we have to reach a point where we say, 'That's enough sadness now it's time to let go.'

The Gesture of Letting Go

Bending your arms at the elbows, raise your hands in front of you, palms facing towards you. Hold for 1 to 2 minutes, eyes closed. Focus your awareness on filling the lungs with white light.

This gesture allows us to let go of old feelings of grief.

Gesture of Silence

To close the senses, place your:
Thumbs in the ears.
Index fingers above the eyebrows.
Middle fingers on the closed eyelids.
Ring fingers at the base of the nasal bone.
Little fingers on the closed lips.
Tongue behind the back of the upper teeth.

188

Breathe in, and on the outbreath - hum!
Perform not more than three times and then simply sit in silence.

This gesture dissolves grief.

Seat of Compassion

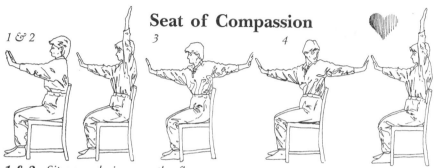

189

1 & 2. Sit on a chair or on the floor. Raise your arms in front to shoulder height, palms forward.

3. Breathe in, raise the left arm up. Breathe out and twist to the left, bringing the arm down behind you.

4. Turn to look at your left hand for a few seconds.

5. Breathe in, raising the left arm back to the vertical. Breathe out, bringing the arm back to meet the other hand. Repeat with the right side.

This sequence opens the heart and helps to release feelings of grief

I have made the frankest admission of my sins,
but I do not carry their burden on my shoulders.

M K Gandhi

*from guilt
to freedom*

The gentle fields of Shropshire became the perfect setting for life's answer to guilt. We had already walked twenty miles along the canal bank when we met a man called Colin who showed us that guilt can be a motivator - a catalyst to move into a positive mode.

He told us that he had been driving along that morning with the radio on when he heard an appeal for the children injured in Rwanda. Their plight was just too much for him, so he stopped his car at the first phone box, rang the Rwandan Aid number and said to them, 'Here is my credit card number - take a thousand pounds and do it quickly before I have time to change my mind!'

He explained that he knew he had to do it instantly, without delay as he would never be able to pluck up the courage to do it after the feeling had left him. Acting spontaneously is following your heart signals, which is crucial to preventing a feeling of not having acted in the right way.

Mansukh

Many people go through life feeling something is 'wrong' with them, or that they have done something 'wrong', perhaps not even knowing what it is.

Children often blame themselves if things go wrong in the family. Perhaps parents split up or a brother or sister has an accident or dies. They may be convinced they are somehow responsible in some way for the pain that is happening around them.

193

Some people have done things that **they are aware of** that makes them feel guilty, but because guilt serves no useful purpose whatsoever, the best thing is still to let it go!

Joy heals everything.

A man once came to Mahatma Gandhi to ask for help. He had personally been responsible for the killing of many children and found himself tormented by guilt both day and night.

Gandhi advised him to go out and find an orphaned child and to bring it up as his own.

194 We all make mistakes in life and **the important thing is to move on.** Whatever we may have done in our life, we may never be able to repair the damage we have caused, but we can resolve to do something really positive to rebalance the situation.

Guilt creates a great restriction around the heart centre. We put boundaries around what we can and cannot do in life because of what has gone before. This restricts our ability to interact with other people.

You could spend your whole life punishing yourself for what you think you have done either real or imagined, or for not being the great person you think you should be; but it only brings pain.

'Guilty' people sabotage their lives because the root thought is, **'I don't deserve'** - to be happy, healthy, rich or successful. They will punish themselves through overeating, undereating, smoking, poverty, illness or having accidents.

195

Even if we have done something 'wrong', we can still decide not to take it on. Because it is a choice.

Just let go of it!

Guilt never made anything better for anyone.

Ask yourself:
1. What have I learned from this?

2. What is there about this experience I could be grateful for?

Action:
196   **1.** Acknowledge you have done something that doesn't match up to your own standard.

2. In your mind, re-enact the situation and see yourself behaving in a way that is in accordance with your own standard.

3. Forgive yourself and let go of the guilt.

4. Be determined not to do it again.

1. Sit in the thunderbolt with joined palms.

2. Breathing in, extend the arms out and raise them above your head, looking up slightly.

3. Breathe out, bending forward from the hips, keeping the back straight. Avoid lifting the hips. Hands touch the ground.

Breath of the Hero

4. Hold this position for a few moments breathing naturally.

5. Breathe in raising up, bringing the arms above the head once again.

6. Breathe out, and come back to the starting position. **Perform at least once every day and up to three times. If you have a heart condition, keep the breath flowing easily and do not hold it at all. Releases burdens.**

197

3 & 4

The Crane Gesture

198

1 & 4 *2a* *2b* *3*

1. Sit with the hands resting on the knees, right palm uppermost.

2. As you breathe in, raise the hands up in front of the face. Separate the hands out and turn them outwards, pressing thumb and index fingers tightly together forming the crane gesture.

3. Hold the gesture tightly for 10 to 15 seconds focussing on the pressure between the thumbs and index fingers.

4. Breathing out, release the gesture, and on the next out breath bring the hands back to the starting position. **This gesture releases guilt.**

Maybe all the pain and all the tragedies
are absolutely essential for us,
so that real contentment,
which is our inherent nature, can flourish.
Learn to work with pain
and turn it to your advantage.

Mansukh

from jealousy
to inner security

Our walk through India followed the route of Gandhi's salt march to Dandi beach. It took us through some of the poorest areas of Navsari city where people crowd into tiny dung-lined huts, with roofs made from a patchwork of old iron sheets, sacks and bags. Children flocked around as their parents laughed and joked with us from their little doorways.

202

Their eyes sparkled so brightly, and although as Westerners we were materially rich beyond all comparison, there was no trace of animosity or jealousy in those eyes. What can we learn from these simple people?

Mansukh

Jealousy can tear people apart inside and be very destructive to a relationship if it is not understood and dealt with. It is a very painful place to be and seems to hit at the very deepest part of us. As people have even been known to kill from this point of pain, it is a great triumph to overcome such a primal emotion.

Primal because it touches the part that desperately needs to survive in a world which we may not feel is abundant - with love, money and resources. If we could truly understand the nature of love, we would not be able to believe this at all.

If the person we love is loving someone else, we may believe our love has run out. If someone at work gets the job we really want we may believe that there will never be a similar chance for us.

So jealousy comes from a belief in scarcity.

Jealousy arises out of two interrelated feelings.

1. From a feeling that someone else is getting what we really feel we want or need in our life. It could be love, money, possessions or prestige, which are all manifestations of our need to feel honoured, respected and valued.

204 **2.** From a feeling of **rejection.** Feeling that we are not good enough, undeserving or inadequate. The truth is that we are only **rejecting ourselves** through a belief in our own inadequacy.

Self-rejection is not considering yourself worthy of being loved or worthy of honour and respect. It comes from a deep sense of insecurity and lack of ability to really love, honour and respect ourselves.

Imagination can play a big part in this emotion. Often we can imagine circumstances that are not even happening. Someone may be late home because they have broken down in the pouring rain with no telephone nearby, but their spouse imagines they are with someone else.

A jealous person will always be searching for something to be jealous of. So it's important not to let the imagination run wild.

205

If you are feeling jealous - you are rejecting yourself.

There was once a man who had such a jealous wife that she spent all her time looking through his pockets, letters and files for evidence of betrayal.

Whenever he came home, she would interrogate him mercilessly, investigate the new telephone numbers in his diary and look for hairs on his coat.

206

One day, she couldn't find a *single hair* on his coat, or any evidence of any kind and she burst into tears. Her husband was amazed. 'What's the matter now?' he said. 'You haven't found a single hair!'

She replied, 'That's why I am upset. You have started going with bald women!'

This is the jealous mind in action!

1. Go outside and find a dandelion seed head. Lie down or squat in front of it. Holding onto the stem, blow the seeds imagining that as all the seeds disperse, your jealousy is also breaking up.

2. Go straight to the mirror and say **'I love you'** over and over again to yourself until you mean it. Give yourself the love you need right now.

3. Forgive the people concerned and try to understand how they are feeling. Realise that everyone is the same inside and wants to feel loved, valued, honoured and respected, the same as you, and is trying to feel that, often in ways we cannot understand!

4. Advanced Heart Power technique:

Think of someone you really love.

Imagine their face.

208

Now superimpose the face of the person towards whom you feel jealousy.

Extend that same love to them.

Yes! It's really hard to do! But it works!

See page 132 - The Mirror Image

Gesture of Inner Security

from the front

*Interlock all the fingers into clasped
hands. Close the eyes and hold for at
least one and a half minutes. Focus
on building security within yourself.*

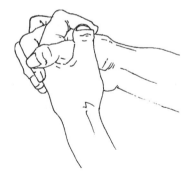

209

This gesture builds inner strength

Joy comes from inside

Blinded at the age of eight in an accident, Jacques Lusseryan
discovered a world of joy and light within himself. He called it his
'secret world' because nobody seemed to understand when he
tried to tell them about it. When the war began and he was only
sixteen he organised a youth resistance movement, enrolling over
200 young people. Using his inner sight he could 'sense' whether
people were trust-worthy or not.

He and his friends were eventually arrested and sent to
Buchenwald. It was here that Jacques contracted pleurisy and was
left to die. As he lay dying he was only aware of one thing. The
breath that came into and out of his body.

**' There was only one thing left which I could do - not to refuse
God's help, which was the breath he was blowing upon me.'**

He experienced that the life he felt within his breath became 'a substance' within him that forced its way into his sickness, with a force a thousand times stronger than he was. It came towards him, 'like a shimmering wave.' It touched him and filled him to overflowing and slowly brought him back to life.

It was the greatest battle he had ever had to face. 'Hard and wonderful all at once.' A battle between the joy that maintains life and the fear that kills.

The flood of joy that he experienced never left him and the next eleven months of extreme wretchedness did not leave a single evil memory on his mind.

The awareness of the power of joy within him was so great that all he could do was try to share it with others and to show them how to hold onto life and to believe in the power of that life.

*P*ain is a part of you
that is waiting for love

Contents

Mastering the Dance - Part II

*S*ome day, after we have mastered the winds,
the waves, the tides and gravity,
we shall harness the energies of love.
Then, for the second time in the history of the world,
man will have discovered fire.

Teilhard de Chardin

Love
the power of
the heart

love

What is love? Love is the part of us that is real, that makes us peaceful, content, happy and free. We feel tolerant, generous and able to open up to people, 'at one' with life and everyone around us.

It is the energy that lies at the core of creation - the primordial force that brings everything into being. It is the very nature of what we call 'life', the great mystery that keeps everything going. It is big! Love is not limited to this or that circumstance or person. Love is everywhere, sustaining everything all the time.

No-one knows where its origin lies, but what we do know is that the human heart is an invisible source of this energy, pouring out great vitality and power. The Institute of HeartMath in California are proving scientifically that there is a massive energy field around the heart that operates at a higher band of frequency than the mind.

Heart power is not new. Ever since man first walked the earth the human heart has been a source of power to him. Amazingly, few people are truly aware of the extraordinary power of love available to them. Heart power has become hidden from us in our 20th century head-orientated society and perhaps that is why stress is the greatest source of disease that we face today.

If love is where we came from and is our true nature, what has happened to mask that feeling from our everyday experience? Why can't we feel it all the time?

Somewhere during our evolution, we have become disconnected from the love that lies within and all around us. We have come to believe that 'love' and 'power' are something **outside of us** and that we need to look for them in people, places and things, like money and prestige.

Believing that love comes from outside and that it is necessary to find someone to be loved by, has disempowered us and cut us off from the power of our own human heart.

We need to recognise that the love we all long for **is already there inside us** and we just have to find ways to feel that love all the time. Then, we must look at what it is we are thinking, feeling and doing that may be masking our true nature from ourselves, and set about making adjustments

Getting in touch with **heart power** means we return to a more natural way of being where love is not a limited commodity, but an unlimited resource within us.

Love has the power to dissolve any negative experience - no matter what it is.

1. One of the best ways to get in touch with love in its purest form is **to give. Generosity** is *the fastest way* to open the heart. It connects us to the very heart of creation which is always giving. To witness this truth, you only have to look at a flower or tree, that grows from one little seed and gives back millions. Creation gives and gives without ever taking **because that is the nature of life.** If you can think of ways to give, you will find your whole experience of life will begin to change.

219

2. Gratitude is another big way to feel your heart power. Actively giving thanks for everything in your life - no matter what it is. Being grateful for the good times and the bad times, the pain and the joy, the laughter and the tears, opens the heart.

3. Sitting quietly with yourself and focussing the mind even for a short time each day puts you in touch with yourself and your own true source of love.

He who binds himself to joy,
doth the winged life destroy,
He who kisses joy as it flies,
lives in eternity's sunrise.

William Blake

Joy
our true nature

Reflect for a moment on the first time in your life that you ever watched the sun rise, or walked along the beach on a warm summer's day, or someone said, **'I love you'.**

> **Holding a tiny kitten or a new born baby.**
> **Seeing a shooting star.**
> **Sitting by a camp fire.**

222

These are all symptoms of the joy we feel when our mind stops 'wanting'. We don't want the moment to be anything other than it is. We have total acceptance of life **as it is** at that time.

The joy we can see in a child's eyes is still there within us, believe it or not! It has simply become buried beneath all sorts of other things. So our task is to uncover our childlike nature and to make that our major focus rather than pain, troubles, stresses and strains.

In the heart of humanity, joy is our natural state of being. So joy is what we seek in every situation.

When we were in the Middle East, for instance, where people are suffering so much oppression, we saw how much they still smile and laugh. Although there is a lot of anguish and pain on both sides, they all feel an urgency to find joyful moments in their lives. There is a buoyancy about them because they instinctively know they need that joy to survive.

So children still laugh and play in the streets, and light fireworks, even though they all live under a constant threat of death.

Joy is a spontaneous outburst from the laughing heart.

The will to live is so powerful and when you confront that power, there are only two ways to go:

Either   You close up and die
Or   You open up like a flower and blossom.

If even one person can rise to their greatness, that capacity exists
224 within the whole of humanity.

Success in this is a matter of **choice.** Our problem is that it is too easy to make pain our focus and allow that to fill our lives. In any situation where life is creating the dance between pain and joy, **we choose what we empower**. Joy is there, but often we put all our attention on to the pain, completely ignoring the presence of its counterpart.

It is just another bad habit we have fallen into. If we can retrain ourselves to look for joy - then, we will find it!

When we can make joy our focus, then joy will expand and fill our lives.

Like the coal miner who was so badly injured in a mining accident that he was completely paralysed from the neck down. When his friends came to visit him at home they were all so focussed on how awful it was that **he** had to cheer **them** up. He said, 'Hey! Do you know what? My toes never get cold any more!'

That's focussing on joy.

*F*orgiveness is the perfume that the trampled flower
casts upon the heel that crushes it.

Forgiveness
the key to happiness

Forgiveness is one of the most powerful tools for healing there is, and perhaps that is why it is so hard to do. Let me repeat that:

Forgiveness is one of the most powerful tools for healing there is.

It can free us from the deepest pain, both physical and emotional - including symptoms of longstanding resentment and bitterness. If it can set us free, why do we find it so hard to do?

228

Perhaps we think that if we forgive someone for something they have done, that somehow we are letting them 'get away with it'. Almost as though our hatred is the punishment we impose upon them.

> **Hatred and non-forgiveness is the punishment**
> **we give to ourselves.**

Non-forgiving not only hurts us, it gradually destroys us.

Rabbi Gelberman lost his whole family during the Nazi holocaust. He witnessed his colleagues bringing Hitler with them to America in their constant expressions of rage and hostility. He saw how their hatred and anger actually killed them and he was determined that Hitler would not get him too.

'I cannot forgive Hitler in the name of my wife, child and parents, but I can choose to feel the joy they were cut off from and entitled to, instead of feeling anger and hostility,' he said. In not being able to forgive Hitler, his colleagues gave him victory. If they had forgiven, victory would have been theirs.

229

So it's not about **deserving** forgiveness or **not deserving** it. The truth is, **we deserve not to suffer** from the painful and harmful effects of non-forgiving.

Why should I forgive?

1. One moment of sincere forgiveness can clear away the debris of years of pain.

2. In forgiveness, you will free yourself from the **burden** of having been wronged.

230

3. If you actively practice forgiveness, it brings the power of the heart to work on the conditioning of your unconscious mind. It can break the self-destructive habits of the emotions of anger, grief and hatred.

4. If you really want to achieve happiness in your life, you must make an effort to forgive those whom you feel have wronged you.

How can I forgive?

Stage 1. Affirm every day: **'I am willing to forgive.'** Work with this affirmation until you find the idea easier to accept.

Stage 2. Practise the Heart Expansion Breath (page 80) every day. This will help to relieve you of the burdens you carry in your life.

Stage 3. Write on a piece of paper everything you feel. All the anger, bitterness and pain. Wrap it around a small twig and gently place it into the river and watch it float away to the sea, taking with it any bitterness or pain.

Stage 4. Visualise the person concerned. You will know when you are ready to do this because you will be able to think about them without reacting negatively.

Look them in the eyes and say, **'I forgive you for what you have
done'**.

Congratulations! You are now free!

A thousand mile journey begins with one step.

M K Gandhi

Hope and freedom

What is missing from our lives? Hope!

The fragrance of hope is all around us, and yet we are unable to grasp or taste it. Why? Because its ways are beyond the comprehension of the ordinary, functional mind. Hope is everywhere - and yet it is nowhere to be seen. We can live without food or water, but we should never try to live without hope.

236   **With hope -** all our dreams and aspirations become possible - because it is the surfboard upon which we ride the triumphs and challenges of our life.

Bring hope into your words, your actions and your vision, because nurturing hope will give shape and meaning to your life.

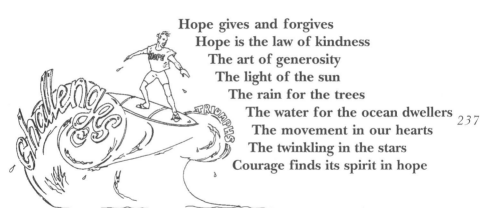

**Hope gives and forgives
Hope is the law of kindness
The art of generosity
The light of the sun
The rain for the trees
The water for the ocean dwellers
The movement in our hearts
The twinkling in the stars
Courage finds its spirit in hope**

237

Hope remains with us always.

This is one of the most inspiring poems that I have ever seen. It is written on a bronze plaque on the wall of the Institute of Physical Medicine and Rehabilitation in New York City. Its author is said to be an unknown federate soldier.

For all those who have suffered and felt the agony and sadness of life, I hope that this poem will bring you faith and comfort. Every time you find life confusing or are at a loss, please read it so that it can set a flame of hope alive in your heart.

238

> **As food is necessary for the body,**
> **prayer is necessary for the soul.**

M K Gandhi

I asked God for strength
that I might achieve,

*I was made weak that I might learn
humbly to obey.*

I asked for health that I
might do great things,

*I was given infirmity that I might do
better things.*

I asked for riches that I
might be happy,

*I was given poverty that I might
be wise.*

I asked for power that I
might have the praise of men,

*I was given meekness that I might feel
the need of God. 239*

I asked for all things that I
might enjoy life,

*I was given life that I might enjoy
all things.*

I got nothing that I asked for
but everything I'd hoped for.

*Almost despite myself my unspoken
prayers were answered.*

I am among men most richly blessed.

The entire world depends upon our actions - here and now. To live for freedom means to **think, talk, dream, act and live freedom.** Exploitation of any kind - at any level of the human community is a symptom of lack of freedom, for our only real freedom lies not just in our knowledge, but more precisely in our 'attainment'. A living desire to improve ourselves **from the centre** for the sake of the whole world community of which we are a part. It's a matter of **'heart culture'** - which means expressing ourselves fearlessly with conviction for what is good and true.

240

We must **believe in freedom** and be willing to live fully for the well-being of our physical, mental, emotional and spiritual strength. The joy and the wonderment freedom brings are borne out of the **deepest faith in the power of life**.

No man loses his freedom except through his own weakness.

M K Gandhi

Why walk 3,000 miles?

It is one thing to have a vision for a better world, but one needs to be able to put power and energy behind that vision.

In our experience, a walking journey takes us far closer to the reality and core of a culture, enabling us to more readily make contact with people at the grass roots level. It is a powerful way of meeting everyday human experience.

Mahatma Gandhi walked to demonstrate his immense commitment to freeing India. The simple human act of placing one foot in front of the other for a length of time creates a tremendous one-pointedness in the mind. Walking enabled him to empower his purpose and to be in touch with the people of India and also allowed them to join him in his journeys and to be inspired by his enthusiasm and purpose.

Gandhi walked with nothing, wearing only a loin cloth, making the statement that each person is complete **as they are** and that the power a human being has, he or she carries within - not in material wealth. Inspired by Gandhi, we are also walking to put energy behind our words and action behind our vision. For we believe that every act we enter into, anchored by very powerful thoughts, really can make a difference.

242

**The miracle is not to fly in the air
or to walk on the water
but to walk on the earth.**

Chinese proverb

The simple additional guidelines below will start to empower a change in your life-style so that you will no longer be a slave to emotions and just reacting to events.

* Make sure you get enough rest and eat good, wholesome food.

* Associate with people that inspire and uplift you.

* Take time to be with yourself and to cultivate silence.

* Just do a little bit every day. Life does not need to be about 100% change all at once. It is more about one hundred 1% changes!

* The more you practice the more Body/Heart/Mind Technology will help you to balance your life.

Acknowledgements

This book would not have been possible without the support and inspiration of many people.

Our heartfelt thanks to Sally Langford, who spent many months researching and compiling information for us, as well as typing, page-setting and designing. To Chris Barrington for his constant encouragement, support, inspiration and advice. To Annie Jones, our Body/Heart/Mind Technology Consultant for all her help and guidance. Thanks to my dear friend Marcel Messing for his foreword and to Dr Helena Waters, Jean McCuish and Andrew Wells for their contributions.

244

To Jean Marvin for hours of starlit and early morning computer stints and her total dedication and love. To all our colleagues at the Life Foundation who have supported our journeys and pilgrimages - too many to mention, but without whom our work would not be possible. It is difficult to express the immense gratitude we feel towards each one of them.

To Regina Doerstel and Jeff Cushing for their advice, inspiration and cover design. Special thanks to Jane Patel, John Jones, Anita Goswami, Paulette Agnew, Barbara Wood, Gordon Turner and Mieke De Graaf for their enthusiasm and creative ideas and for making our lives easier. For hours of proof reading, we must thank Anne and Emily Douglas, Gwyneth Clapham and Ruth Boaler.

To Lucy Claire Byatt we extend our deepest thanks for her skill in illustration. She has the ability to produce drawings at the drop of a hat, and with such enthusiasm and cheerfulness that it makes her a joy to work with. May we thank all the wonderful people we have met on our journeys, again too many to mention. They have each one enriched our lives and expanded our vision for a better world. Last but not least we thank Mahatma Gandhi for his inspiration and guidance through example.

Thank you

Dr Mansukh Patel

A rare combination of scientist, philospher, author, teacher and therapist. Growing up as a child in the wilds of the Rift Valley in Kenya has been a perfect training ground for understanding life in its deepest and truest sense. Witnessing the Mau Mau uprising at first hand, he has been exposed to life in its rawest form. His knowledge of pain and human suffering is therefore profound and has given him a deep compassion for the human predicament.

246

In later years he has combined his study of biochemistry and research into cancer toxicology, with osteopathy and knowledge from many traditions. The result is a wealth of practical techniques and wisdom that really works for people.

A 'man of his heart', Mansukh feels deeply that every individual holds within them the key to their own freedom. His immense compassion for people and the environment has inspired him to instigate and actively follow through many outstanding and unique projects including the Friendship Without Frontiers pilgrimage, LifeWalk 2000 and EuroWalk 2000. Inspired by Mahatma Gandhi who truly understood the power of walking, these projects bring hope and inspiration to people all over the world. As one of the founder members of the Life Foundation School of Therapeutics, his greatest joy has always been to teach people how to live in a joyful, creative and successful way, no matter what trials and tribulations they face.

Mansukh is based in North Wales where he lives with his wife Jane and their three beautiful children.

Rita Goswami BA (Hons)
A woman with a vision and the energy to see it through. Rita was born in Africa in the fifties and brought up in an atmosphere of military confrontation. She too, has been exposed to the deepest

human issues from a very early age. Becoming aware of a prevalence of prejudice instigated a very deep inner search for solutions to the problems that beset us all. She became an advice worker specialising within the ethnic minority groups in the community. She qualified as a nurse after graduating in Sociology at the University College of North Wales in Bangor.

Her care and compassion for people and the extreme suffering she could see all around her led her into the world of yoga and meditation and a personal awakening. Rita has travelled extensively, teaching and promoting her unique approach to self mastery, and most recently led the Friendship Without Frontiers world pilgrimage   promoting inner and outer peace. The journey took 18 months and visited 31 countries.

Rita has the knack of always highlighting the truth in every situation. She has the clarity to perceive and negotiate life with tremendous grace and ease. Her capacity for empathy with others puts her directly in touch with modern day human issues. She draws upon a wealth of knowledge based in Dru Yoga, Holistic Health Care, modern medicine and the Eastern Sciences. Rita is one of the founder members of the Life Foundation School of Therapeutics and is based in the West Midlands at their head office.

The Life Foundation School of Therapeutics (L.F.S.T.) is working to promote the commonness in all peoples and to transcend the boundaries that separate them. It believes that diversity and individuality can be combined to support the truth that all paths are one.

L.F.S.T. aims to apply universal principles, whether physiological or spiritual to day to day living that allows the 'naturalness' of a human being to be expressed and positively directed. L.F.S.T. is looking forward to the 21st century and invites you to take part in its courses and international conferences to explore a lifestyle which is ecologically harmonious and progressive.

Publications are available on request for home study on topics ranging from stress management and self discovery to ecological and environmental issues.

Appendix

Your personal guide to transforming emotional energy in the body

Appendix

Part of Body	Emotion	Colour	Stone	Essential Oil
Heart	Lack of joy/denial	Red	Rose quartz	Jasmine
Liver	Anger/jealousy	Green	Jasper	Chamomile
Gall bladder	Bitterness/resentment	Dark green	Malachite	Lemon
Kidneys	Fear/anxiety	Navy blue	Tourmaline	Geranium
Lungs	Grief/sadness	White	Aventurine	Rose
Knees/hips	Fear of moving on	Green		Clary sage
Neck/joints	Stubborness/rigid thoughts	Turquoise	Blue lace	Sandalwood
Eyes	Perception	Indigo	Lapis	Rosemary
Thyroid	Self expression/creativity	Royal blue	Aquamarine	Blue chamomile
Spleen	Lack of trust in self	Yellow	Jasper	Vetiver
Bladder	Anxiety/holding on	Navy	Citrine	Rose
Pancreas	No sweetness in life	Yellow	Sulphur	Orange
Central Nervous System	Agitated mind	Deep blue	Sodalite	Basil

252

Appendix

Sound	Walking Therapy	Affirmation
OO	Coastal paths	I honour the wisdom of my heart
CHA	By a river	I let go and flow like a river
MMMM	In the rain	I forgive the past and let it go
SHH	Under the stars	I am safe, life is on my side
WAA	In the mountains	I accept everything and let go the past
VAA	By waterfalls	I allow my life to unfold naturally
OOAA	Hill walking	I see life from all viewpoints
HAA	By the sea	I now perceive life as it really is
OHH	In the wind	It is now safe to express myself fully
THAA	Hot sunny days	I believe in my own power
RAA	By canals	Letting go makes room for the new
FA	By waterfalls	I am totally in control of my life
EEE	By still pools	I breathe in calm, I breathe out anxiety

Technique for transforming emotional energy in the body

for heart and lungs

*for
stomach
digestive organs
liver
gall bladder
kidneys
spleen
pancreas*

Using the two middle fingers of the right hand, describe 9 anti-clockwise circles and 7 clockwise circles around the areas indicated. (Direction as if a clock face is drawn on your body.)

*For throat and head problems, we recommend **The Pigeon Breath** and **The Pendulum Meditation**, available on tape or video.*

254

Other books by Dr Mansukh Patel

The Peace Formula
The Inside Story
Come With Me
Ancient Teachings for Modern Living

Printed on **Savannah**,
an environmentally friendly paper produced from sugar cane.